D1125747

Married
to the
Military

A Survival Guide for
Military Wives, Girlfriends,
and Women in Uniform

Meredith Leyva

CinC💮House.com

The Internet's Largest Community of Military Wives and Women in Uniform

A Fireside Book
Published by Simon & Schuster
New York London Toronto Sydney

Fireside
A Division of Simon & Schuster, Inc.
1230 Avenue of the Americas
New York, NY 10020

Copyright © 2003, 2009 by Meredith Leyva

This Fireside trade paperback edition July 2009

FIRESIDE and colophon are registered trademarks
of Simon & Schuster, Inc.

For information about special discounts for bulk purchases,
please contact Simon & Schuster Special Sales at
1-866-506-1949 or business@simonandschuster.com.

The Simon & Schuster Speakers Bureau can bring authors to your live event. For more information or to book an event contact the Simon & Schuster Speakers Bureau at 1-866-248-3049 or visit our website at www.simonspeakers.com.

Designed by Elliott Beard

Manufactured in the United States of America

10 9 8 7

Library of Congress Cataloging-in-Publication Data
Leyva, Meredith
    Married to the military: a survival guide for military wives, girlfriends, and women in uniform / Meredith Leyva.
        p.   cm.
    Includes index.
    1. Military spouses—United States—Handbooks, manuals, etc.
2. Families of military personnel—United States—Handbooks, manuals, etc.
3. United States—Armed Forces—Military life—Handbooks, manuals, etc.
I. Title.
U766.L49   2009
    355.1'2—dc22   2009007167

ISBN 978-1-4391-5026-9
ISBN 978-1-4165-9322-5 (ebook)

CONTENTS

12 What Happens When the Worst Happens—and What to Do   177

13 Preventing Trouble in Paradise   187

14 Really Stupid Acronyms and Jargon   190

Married
to the
Military

CHAPTER 1

Welcome *to the* Adventure *of* Military Life!

Welcome to the sisterhood of military women! We are military wives, girlfriends, moms, and women in uniform. Just like you, we had to familiarize ourselves with military life and get to know the community pretty darn quick, sometimes while getting engaged and planning a wedding and other times while reeling from the shock of our Reservist husband suddenly being sent off to war. With all the crazy acronyms, rules, and bureaucracy on top of finding bridesmaids' dresses, it's easy to get overwhelmed—but don't! You can master this, and we are here to help you.

In effect, this book is an orientation manual on military life based on the collective knowledge of military wives and women at CinCHouse .com. CinCHouse.com is the Internet's largest community of military women all over the world. In fact, the name "CinCHouse" is military jargon for "Commander *in* Chief of the House." That's what you are! And don't you forget it.

You are the CinC of your house because, while your husband is out playing G.I. Joe, you are primarily responsible for raising the kids, managing the household finances, and establishing yourself and your family in the community. This is no job for the faint of heart. Don't be deceived by the feminine looks of many military wives standing next to their macho men; underneath lies the heart of Scarlett O'Hara. Besides, although the military may joke that "if we wanted a service member to have a wife, we would have issued one," your needs and personal and professional goals are just as important as your man's.

Just remember this cardinal rule: Success in military life is all about knowledge and perspective. The purpose of this book is to give you information and a well-rounded perspective on military life so that you can make the right choices for yourself and your family, especially if you are starting a new life as a military wife. This book will:

> Introduce you to daily life in the military and what you can expect in terms of services and the community—and what is expected of you.
> Help you understand the benefits and how to get the most out of military life (the business of your marriage).
> Help you understand and take control of the two primary threats to your sanity: relocation and deployment.
> Strengthen your marriage by helping you develop a strategy with your service member on how to live together.

Dealing with Jargon, Political Correctness, and Other Nonsense

Unfortunately, military jargon has become a language all its own. You can refuse to learn it and find yourself corrected or stuck not knowing what was said, or you can become familiar with the basics. We prefer the latter approach, although we limit our use of jargon as much as possible. After all, our hubbies signed up for the job, not us.

To help you through, every time a new acronym is introduced, we write it out fully and explain what it means. We explain military jargon in the same manner. Chapter 14 is a glossary entitled "Really Stupid Acronyms and Jargon" for your reference. The glossary is also good for translating lingo when on base, especially with the die-hard Marines.

Also, let's skip the political correctness and just acknowledge that this

WAR STORIES

Help, I Need to Talk!

I was working 14 hours a day in Washington, D.C., at a high-powered corporate public relations agency when my husband first joined the military. Although most of the wives at our command worked, the spouse club was run by stay-at-home moms. That meant most meetings and social events consisted of hours of lunch and bingo or mom 'n' tot play groups.

My girlfriends and I needed more information about military life and what was in store for us. The command was threatening to relocate our families all over the place. Our lives felt completely out of control, and we didn't have a clue how to work the system. However, we also didn't have time to participate in spouse club events and, very frankly, we resented being left out. So did the female service members in our command who wanted to hang out with fellow girlfriends. So we jimmied up a website with a discussion forum that allowed us to talk during the day at work or late at night after the kids went to bed.

Apparently we weren't the only ones who felt this way, because the website had 40,000 hits in the first month of its existence. By 2003, that little website received nearly 900,000 visits each month. Thus was the birth of CinCHouse.com.

book is written primarily for women, namely military wives and women in uniform. The Department of Defense (**DoD**) is required to use the term "spouse," but we use the more accurate term "wife." While the number of military husbands has increased slightly, they still represent only 7 percent of all military spouses, and the vast majority previously served in the military and are already very familiar with it. That is very different from a 20-something civilian woman who is just entering or marrying into the military for the first time. We are women, and we want to act and be treated as such.

Additionally, this book takes a fresh approach by recognizing that women in uniform and military wives have common concerns. While military wives are primarily addressed because there are so many of us, many female service members will find it useful because they share the same responsibilities for raising kids and managing households, finances, and relocation. There are plenty of orientation books on military jobs and protocol, but there are almost no good books about handling the family and personal aspects of military life. Thus, the term "military wife" also refers to those female service members who feel married to the military and want solutions to these issues.

Finally, before I get hate mail from nitpickers, let me say that this book covers the *general concepts* behind key aspects of military life. Different military services, bases, and offices, however, will do things slightly differently. Form 840 on Base A may be referred to as Form 850 on Base B, even though they say the same thing. The two forms are just printed on different-colored paper. What the Navy calls a "detailer" the Army calls a "branch manager"—but they do the same thing. What is important is that the concepts are the same, and this book will give you the tools to get through them. It is not intended to be a bible to address every situation under the sun.

Your husband, boyfriend, or fiancé may freak out when he sees you reading this book. Why on earth, he'll say, do you need to understand this stuff? He'll take care of everything! And he can explain what you do need to know when you need to know it. Right?

Wrong! You need to know about military life so you can control your family's destiny, and he may not always be around to explain how things work or to handle the situation. Your gut instinct tells you that. What you *can* tell your man is that, by reading this book, you will feel better about entering the adventures of military life, and you will be better able to support him in his mission and have a stronger relationship.

The Least You Need to Know

> ▸ You are neither the first nor the last woman to face the complicated world of military life.

> This book is designed to help you succeed in taking control of your destiny and strengthening your relationship with your service member.
> The key to controlling your destiny is to learn about military life, including all its acronyms and jargon.

RESOURCE

> www.cinchouse.com—The Internet's largest community of military wives and women in uniform.

CHAPTER 2

Your First Day *as* CinCHouse

Getting Documented

Your first "day" in the military starts with getting proper documentation. If you're a service member, you will be walked through most of this, including how to get your family's documentation completed. As a wife, especially one of a Reservist, you need to make sure your service member takes care of the following:

› *Submitting a marriage packet to his command's administration.* No documentation is more important because with it you will be officially recognized and receive the benefits of a spouse by the Defense Enrollment Eligibility Reporting System (**DEERS**). As a wife, you will be able to shop at the commissary, receive life insurance benefits if your service member dies, and obtain health care virtually free of cost. As a girlfriend or fiancée, you get squat. Similarly, a married service member receives a substantial increase in pay, but none of it kicks in until the paperwork is submitted. This is why many couples choose a courthouse wedding before a deployment and organize a "real" wedding upon his return. Without that marriage certificate, the fiancée is left behind with no rights or benefits.

❯ *Obtaining a military spouse identification card.* A spouse's military I.D. card obtained from the personnel office (DD Form 1172, "Application for Uniformed Services Identification Card") looks like a brown driver's license. You will be asked for this I.D. every time you pay for groceries, work out at the base gym, arrive for a doctor's appointment, or go to the bathroom (well, not really). In times of heightened security (referred to as "**threatcon**" or "threat condition"), you will be required to show your I.D. to the guard before entering the base. No I.D., no access without a ton of interrogation and paperwork, even if you live in base housing.

❯ *Obtaining a base decal for your car.* A decal from the base security office tells the gate guards and military police that you are allowed to be on base until the expiration date listed on the decal. It also tells them whether the car owner is enlisted or an officer, and officers' cars are typically saluted by the gate guard, even if the spouse is driving. (They're saluting the officer or NCO rank indicated on the decal, silly, not you!) Most guard gates require only a decal to allow your car on base. However, if you have an I.D. but no decal, they will hassle you and insist on seeing your car registration, insurance, and other documents stuck to your glove compartment with old gum you left there. Better to be able to whiz through instead of always having to fish out your military I.D. and other documents (car registration and insurance) from the depths of your purse and glove compartment.

❯ *Entering you into Tricare.* **Tricare** is the military's very own HMO. Although we address health care in more depth later on, what's important is that you get signed up and assigned a primary care physician so that you have access to virtually free health care at any time, particularly in an emergency. Don't wait for a car accident before you sign up, or you'll be recuperating in a bureaucratic nightmare.

❯ *Obtaining a Power of Attorney.* A Power of Attorney, or **POA,** may seem like a big deal, but it's standard equipment for military families. Basically, a POA allows you to conduct business on behalf of your service member in his absence, namely during deployments, but it also helps when he's out on training missions and can't be reached. Do not wait for an unanticipated deployment to get your POA. You never know when an event like September 11 will happen and your husband will call you to say he's shipping out in five minutes, see you in six months. Without a POA, you will have no other way to deal with financial institutions, apply for base housing, or do any number of things you never think about when he's around. This means, for example, that you will not be able to take cash out of his banking accounts even if you need it desperately to pay the rent. Banks especially are sticklers on this.

Did You Know?

Military service members receive a substantial increase in pay when they get married! The difference is as little as $100 and as much as several thousand dollars per month in extra income. But don't make the mistake many couples do and go overboard with family planning. You don't get an extra cent for having kids (unless the service member is a single parent).

If your hubby deploys having accomplished none of these tasks, he can still obtain a POA from the Judge Advocate General (**JAG**). Written correctly—with express powers given to you for each need—that POA can get your financial account access, military I.D. card, Tricare enrollment, and so on. Your hubby has an administrative command stationed back home to take care of exactly these kinds of issues, so work with them to get the POA and the process straightened out.

Your service member may also want to go to the base legal office to write a will. This is a particularly good idea if you have kids or are remarried, but it's not absolutely necessary in the beginning. Having said that, I have seen families go broke because a service member's "estate" (benefits) was tied up in Probate Court for eight months. As with

WAR STORIES

He's at Sea and I Have No Money!

I can't tell you how many times a freaked-out wife has come to me saying she can't access any of the bank accounts or credit cards and has no money even to buy groceries, much less pay rent. Why? The couple got married in a hurry or were otherwise too busy to put the service member's bank accounts in both names. That was no problem when he was home because he could just write a check for the rent or pull out cash from the ATM. But when he left, the wife no longer had access to his bank accounts. Had she had a POA, she could have accessed the accounts or even had the military finance system direct-deposit the service member's pay into her checking account. Similar crises have occurred when a couple is finally accepted into base housing, but the wife does not have a POA to sign the papers on the service member's behalf. The couple loses their spot on the housing list after waiting months to get to the top. The moral of this story: Get a POA now!

a POA, creating a will takes an hour or less and is totally free of charge at the JAG. You might as well make a will while getting a POA.

Now that you have your to-do list, the first thing you should know is that the official military bureaucracy generally views wives as second-class citizens. That's actually okay. Their first priority should be to care for the service members, who have literally sworn their lives to protecting the United States. (No kidding! Just ask your hubby about his oath.) Then come the family members, and then come the veterans.

Unfortunately, another reason for this second-class treatment is that other military wives have tried to cheat their husbands by cheating the system, which has forced the military to tighten up regulations, preventing us from doing certain things without the express consent of the service member in person or by POA. While there have been only a handful of scams, they've made for great cocktail party stories among the bureaucracy, and most of them pertain to housing, relocation, and pay. Most of them also have to do with a wife milking everything out of her husband before she leaves him.

Did You Know?

If your service member says he doesn't have time during the day to complete important administrative tasks, make sure he goes through his chain of command to get time off. He is required to do these things, and military regulations specifically give him time off to do them. Besides, his command should understand because they have to do them, too.

If you're one of these wives, be forewarned: They know you're coming. And you stink for lousing things up for the rest of us.

The final reason the bureaucracy may treat you badly is because it's just plain tradition to treat women like "little ladies." The good news is that they will call you "ma'am" and open doors for you. The bad news is that you will find your intentions and intelligence being questioned. And you'll find yourself being called a "dependent," which is an old-fashioned but insulting term for what officially is now designated a "family member."

The bottom line is that this second-class treatment can inhibit your ability to get business done on base, and it totally prevents you from obtaining proper documentation without the assistance of your service member.

Your service member can do all these things a lot more quickly and efficiently than you can—so just send him! You have enough on your to-do list without adding these mind-numbing tasks to it. However, as you can see, it's absolutely critical you make sure he completes them. In fact, it's worth harassing him a bit to make sure he has completed his tasks.

Getting to Know Your Base

As you're getting your documentation and running errands on base, take a look around and get to know what services are available to you and where they are located. Some bases are absolutely huge, so get a map at the guard gate and take the time to drive around. Besides finding out where all the great shopping is, you might get to see tanks whizzing by, Cobra helicopters in battle formation, and all kinds of other thrilling stuff that makes for good cocktail party stories.

Did You Know?

A military I.D. gives you access to any U.S. military base—Army, Navy, Air Force, Marines, or Coast Guard—with the exception of a few high-security bases.

Every base pretty much has the same stuff, but smaller bases have smaller buildings. The **Exchanges** (or military-run department stores) and affiliated specialty stores might become your new hangouts. Each military service has a different name for its department store, but they are all intended to provide savings for military shoppers and basic needs for military families overseas. The Exchanges also put their profits toward the morale programs on base, which you will come to know and love, so it's worth patronizing them whenever possible. The Army calls it the **PX** for "Post Exchange"; the Air Force calls it the **BX** for "Base Exchange"; the Marine Corps calls it the **MCX** for "Marine Corps Exchange"; and the Navy and Coast Guard simply call it the "Exchange." Except for the Navy's all the Exchanges are operated by the Army and Air Force Exchange Service or **AAFES** (pronounced "a-fees"), so you might want to get used to that name, too.

Similarly, the **commissary** (the military-run grocery store), which is run by the Defense Commissary Agency, or **DeCa**, subsidizes the cost of food for military families, particularly on baby items.

Other great family services are provided by the Morale, Welfare, and

Recreation (**MWR**) division of the military—sometimes called the Air Force Services Agency (**AFSA**) in that service—including free health clubs with the latest aerobics classes and equipment, free or discounted entertainment and resort tickets from the Information, Tickets, & Tours (**ITT**) office, and rentals of outdoor, camping, and party equipment for next to nothing. We've even seen activities such as surfing classes, hobby shops, and kids' summer camps organized and promoted by MWR, so be sure that you get a monthly update on what's available by checking your base newspaper.

Did You Know?

While the Exchanges are never as good as Macy's, they are known for killer deals on a few luxury product lines, including Coach leather goods, Estée Lauder and Clinique makeup, and Waterford crystal. Other products and services are available from local vendors near the Exchange, but this is not a mall. You really have to look for bargains.

Speaking of which, your base newspaper can typically be found outside any major public area on base such as the commissary and Exchange. Sometimes it can also be found online on the official website of your base. It is published weekly by the base Public Affairs Office (**PAO**), and contains oodles of information about activities, interest clubs, spouse clubs, and even classified ads. Since there's no cost, you might as well make a habit of picking it up every time you get a chance to find out what's happening near you.

Finally, you need to know where the family support offices can be found, even if you never expect to need their help. Inevitably, you will need to find them for something at least twice during your stay, and it's usually in an emergency or when you're pressed for time. We'll discuss these services later in more detail, but you should at least be able to locate the following:

> Personal Property Office (**PPO**) or Traffic Management Office (**TMO**)
> Legal office
> Hospital or health care clinic
> Family Support Center
> Child Development Center (a.k.a. child care)
> The Navy–Marine Corps Relief Society, Air Force Aid Society, or Army Emergency Relief

Joining the Club

As you finish your paperwork, read the base newspaper, meet the command, and keep an eye out for spouse groups. Every command or unit typically has either an officer spouse club, an enlisted spouse club, or a combined club called a Family Readiness Group (**FRG**). The entire base is also likely to have an all-unit officers' spouses club and enlisted spouses club. The commands have contact information on these groups which they can share with you, and the base newspaper often advertises their events. Often these groups have their own websites as well. Successful wives frequently inquire even before relocating so they can ask questions before the move and then literally walk into a new group of friends.

The Least You Need to Know

> To get the benefits you are entitled to, your service member must do five important things: submit a marriage packet to his command, obtain a military I.D. card for you, put a base decal on your car, enter you in the Tricare system, and grant you a Power of Attorney.
> The bureaucracy for obtaining these items is irritating, so let your husband take care of it—and nag him like his mother until he follows through.
> Before your service member deploys and leaves you to fend for yourself, take the time to drive around the base and familiarize yourself with the services and resources available to you.

RESOURCES

> www.commissaries.com—Find out the latest specials at your base commissary.

> www.aafes.com and www.navy-nex.com—Purchase items from the Exchanges online or find out what's on sale.

CHAPTER 3

Controlling Your Family's Destiny

Understanding your hubby's job is not only important for good marital communication, it is also key to coping with the twin obstacles of relocation and deployment. By **relocation** we mean moving the entire family from one city to another, anywhere in the world, so that your hubby can take up a new tour of duty at a new military base. **Deployment** is when the service member leaves his family and goes out on a mission for an extended period of time, typically six months to one year. During wartime, some units deploy for as long as 18 months, and there is sometimes no telling when exactly they will be able to return home.

Temporary Duty (**TDY** or **TAD**) is extended training periods—for example, going to war games for two weeks, "work ups" testing a ship in preparation for deployment, or attending Advanced Individual Training (**AIT**) at another base for less than 20 weeks. This presents its own problems because sometimes the service member comes and goes almost at random, throwing the family schedule out of whack.

Military wives and female service members with families generally try to avoid relocation and deployment because it causes stress on the family. While short absences make the heart grow fonder, long absences can lead to loneliness, guilt, or resentment for being left behind as a single parent. Unfortunately, many service members don't feel the same way about relocation and deployment. As overgrown Boy Scouts, this breed of service member loves running around with tanks and artillery in the middle of 104°F Middle Eastern heat for months on end. Plus, this is the main reason why they get paid.

You should expect and respect the fact that at some point your service member will be deployed and your family will relocate, possibly at the same time. The key is learning to control your destiny to the extent you can by understanding the military system and choosing a strategy that works best for your family. This chapter will teach you about the military system; chapter 10, entitled "Marriage Hoo-ah," will guide you in developing your own family strategy.

Getting Started in the Military

With rare exceptions, most service members and Reservists begin their new careers by attending basic training and technical schools (such as AIT) if they are enlisted, and Officer Candidate/Training School (**OCS/OTS**), Officer Indoctrination School (**OIS**), Reserve Officer Training Command (**ROTC**), or a service academy (for example, the Air Force Academy and the Citadel) as officers. Enlisted service members going through basic training are referred to as "recruits" and are not considered real service members until they pass; officers-to-be are referred to as "officer candidates."

All of these training programs require service members to leave their families for six weeks to six months, and some are more rigorous than others. The most rigorous programs, such as Marine Corps boot camp, have strict rules about what recruits can keep with them, so be sure to get a list of approved items from the boot camp command before your service member goes. It can be very embarrassing—and will probably add more physical difficulties to your man's training program—if you send him an unapproved item and he gets caught. You don't want dirty pictures of you passed around the camp, and the instructors or recruits will inevitably find the restricted item and make an example out of your man.

WAR STORIES

The Simplest Thing Can Lead to Big Trouble at Boot Camp

After carefully reading the boot camp instructions and talking to other wives, my girlfriend Carrie was determined to send her boyfriend a simple care package that would not get him in trouble. Her care package consisted of homemade cookies (good for buttering up his drill sergeant and fellow recruits) and a few pictures of her with his parents, topped with little sparkles and confetti. Unfortunately, when her boyfriend ripped open the package, the confetti flew everywhere, and little sparkles found their way into every crevice of the wooden floors of his bunk room. As a result, the boyfriend was forced to deep-clean the floors—but only after doing unlimited push-ups.

All basic training rules about phone calls, family visits, graduation, and restricted items should be obtained directly from the basic training command, and they will probably arrive in an information packet before the service member leaves. Many wives, previously familiar with their man's schedule, get desperate for information about exactly when he can call home and when family can visit. Forget about having that kind of control—seriously. The bottom line is that basic training owns your man until graduation day, which is about the only time you will see him. It's a bit of a shock entering military life this way, but the best thing you can do is let your man focus on passing basic training by giving him praise and encouragement instead of nagging and complaints. If he doesn't pass, he'll have to do it all over again unless he's flat kicked out.

Your military pay will kick in during basic training, but you won't start getting a check until 4 to 8 weeks after he starts. Be prepared to have no money until that point, and don't bug his command about it until you've waited at least 4 weeks. You will learn more about pay later on, but note for now that if you are married you will receive Basic Allowance for Housing (**BAH**) as part of his pay. If you're not married, he does not get

Did You Know?

The new post-9/11 GI Bill allows service members to transfer their benefits to a spouse or dependent children under certain conditions, some of which are still being determined as of this writing. The new rules go into effect on August 1, 2009. To be eligible to transfer to a spouse or child, a member must:

» Have served at least six years in the Armed Forces on the date of election and agree to serve four additional years from that date; or

» Have at least 10 years of service in the Armed Forces on the date of election and be precluded from committing to four additional years by law or Service/DoD policy. For example, service members subject to high-year tenure rules and who have 10 years' service at the time of election would be eligible.

» Members who are currently retirement-eligible or who will become retirement-eligible during the period August 1, 2009, through August 1, 2012, also can qualify. "Retirement-eligible" means completion of 20 years of active federal service or completion of 20 years' reserve. Here's how the program will work for various cohorts of retirement eligibles:

› For those eligible to retire on or before August 1, 2009, no additional service is required.

› For those eligible for retirement after August 1, 2009, and before July 1, 2010, one year additional service is required.

› For those eligible for retirement after August 1, 2010, and before July 1, 2011, two years' additional service is required.

› For those eligible for retirement after August 1, 2011, and before July 1, 2012, three years' additional service is required.

Source: Information is courtesy of the Military Officers Association of America.

BAH. Additionally, BAH is determined by the zip code where *you* reside, not where boot camp or AIT is, and it will continue from that point forward until he finishes his training and you relocate to be with him.

Did You Know?

A Job Guy is the military's version of God in terms of determining your family's destiny, so treat him as such. Some Job Guys are more overworked than others, and most Job Guys actually care about the service members they serve—even if they really hate their jobs (most do because of the pressure to make everyone happy). Have pity on this poor soul, but communicate with him. Never yell at him or constantly insist on which duty stations you want. Pry him for intelligence (or "intel") on what duty stations are most likely to be available, and do some horse trading. Some Job Guys hold back on cushy jobs to reward people who are nice to them or who were given bad duty stations in the past. By communicating and being nice to your Job Guy, you're most likely to get the duty stations you want.

The service member's career track is typically determined in the middle of basic training, and additional training such as tech school is likely required. He probably won't receive orders to attend that school until 1–2 weeks before graduation. Schools are less strict in terms of family interaction, and, again, each training command will give you detailed instructions regarding family interaction. If the training program is more than 20 weeks, it may be possible for the service to relocate your family to be with him. But don't assume anything—always check your orders for an explicit statement, or you may be on the hook for the cost of moving, or in trouble. If the information is not provided, ask the command administrator (or "admin") so you don't break any rules but enjoy every opportunity to see each other. This is not basic training, so your hubby should not be embarrassed about asking when it will be appropriate to spend time with family.

Once your hubby passes training, he will be assigned to someone who is responsible for helping him determine his career track and assigning him orders to a new **duty station** (also known as "tour," "billet," or "post" but always referring to a specific job). The duty station also indicates the location of his job. That person in charge of your service member's career is called a **branch manager** (Army) or **detailer** (Navy), among other words (sometimes less kind). Because I can't satisfy every military branch, I will henceforth refer to this person as the "**Job Guy.**" However, you should get accustomed to using the term suitable for your branch. You need to be able to say things like:

> "My husband's detailer offered him a one-year tour in Iraq or a billet on board a ship. Either way he deploys, I want our duty station to be near my parents so they can help me take care of the kids while he's gone."

Understanding Career Tracks

One of the most important things you can learn about the military is that the more special skills your service member acquires, the more pay and career options he gets. Whether it's aviation mechanics school or college, educational opportunities are some of the truly great benefits in the military, and your family should take advantage of them.

Not only is the education paid for (while he continues to receive a salary), he also may get even more pay when he passes and goes to work with his new skills. Further, you and your service member can choose career tracks that improve your chances of meeting family goals, such as relocating to specific places (whether it's back home to your family or a coveted spot in Hawaii) or limiting how often your service member is required to deploy. For example, hospital administrative staff are used mainly at base hospitals or clinics, so they are less likely to deploy and more likely to have a better selection of duty stations to choose from. By contrast, corpsmen and military police are very likely to deploy.

This is true for National Guard and Reserve as well. While originally designed to replace active duty service members in their U.S.-based jobs, many Guard and Reserve are being deployed directly to combat jobs—especially those in high-demand fields. During Operation Iraqi Freedom (**OIF**) and Operation Enduring Freedom (**OEF**), deployment rates for Guard and Reserve reached as high as 50 percent.

Finally, your husband's choice of career track will ultimately determine the type of job he will qualify for when he decides to leave the military—which he will eventually do, no matter how often he wears his combat boots to bed. The reality is that an infantryman may do all kinds of fun stuff in the field, but in the civilian world he may be qualified only for security jobs such as the local police force or highway patrol. A computer programmer, however, can walk out of the military into a six-figure salary if he plays his cards right.

For these reasons, deciding on a career track is a decision for the whole family, and it's important that you research and discuss the options in partnership with your hubby. Find out what his interests are; search the Web to identify training schools and locations; and, most important, work closely with and ask questions of his Job Guy. Leaving your hubby's career track to the winds of fortune is asking for trouble. An indecisive hubby will be the first to deploy, the last to return, and the most likely to be stationed in Diego Garcia (if you don't know where that is, use your imagination).

The Daily Grind

Each military job falls under a "command" or "unit" (i.e., department), and each command has its own rules and administration. Most of your hubby's paperwork (such as "Page 2" of his service record, which enters you officially as a spouse) is submitted through his command admin.

Although the military's hours of operation typically run from 7:30 A.M. to 4:30 P.M., each command may operate on some variation of those hours and require service members to do night watch. Many commands require the service members to get up at o' dark thirty for **PT** (physical training). Obviously, little details like this can make a big difference in a three-year tour, so it's important to check these things out when reviewing duty stations with the Job Guy.

WAR STORIES

Why Recruiters' Jobs Are Considered Worse than Deployment

You would think that after years of being deployed to places like Bosnia, Talia's husband would have been thrilled to get a post as a recruiter near their hometown of Tallahassee. Certainly, their parents were thrilled when they heard the news. But the family quickly learned that recruiters often spend late nights in the office cajoling last-minute walk-ins into joining the Army. Talia couldn't plan a romantic evening or a family dinner because she couldn't count on her hubby to be home. Their parents couldn't understand why he didn't just leave at 5:00 P.M. Talia's husband stayed at the office because of the tremendous pressure to make the monthly quotas of recruits. And he hated "selling" the Army and feeling the need to be less than forthright about some of the hardships. The couple were thrilled when a post opened with a supply unit, even though it meant more deployments to Bosnia.

Deployment schedules and workups are other critical items. They vary not only from service to service and command to command, but also from job to job. And the deployment schedule touted by the command does not always jibe with the real deployment schedule. For example, folks serving on surface ships such as aircraft carriers are supposed to deploy for six months and return for 18 months, but these days they are more likely to deploy for seven to nine months and have less shore time. Additionally, during the six months before deployment they are often at sea doing workups (preparing the ship and conducting qualification drills). Workups drive families crazy because they are unpredictable, pulling the service member out for two weeks, then back for an unspecified time, and then out again.

By contrast, pilots sometimes spend less time on deployment because they can simply fly home when they are no longer needed. And certain jobs, such as in computers, may not require the service member to participate in workups. So whenever possible, talk to your service member's colleagues and supervisors in that career track or who have had that prospective duty station before choosing to accept it. Oftentimes you can also find the same information from wives on the discussion boards of CinCHouse.com and other Internet sites.

The Reality of Relocation

The frequency of relocation and the duration of each assignment are determined by your hubby's career track and specific duty station. The average military family relocates every three years, and approximately 80 percent live in the Continental United States (**CONUS**). Of the 20 percent who live overseas, or **OCONUS**, most live on a variety of bases scattered throughout Western Europe and Japan. Some service members, however, are assigned to "unaccompanied" tours (i.e., they cannot officially bring their families) in remote locations such as South Korea or Guantánamo Bay, Cuba.

Although unaccompanied tours are typically only one year, the military has begun to recognize the damage these duty stations can do to a family, chiefly the emotional isolation that can lead to divorce, and whenever possible they are making more accommodations for families in exchange for longer tour durations. You should recognize the possible damage of unaccompanied tours, too. In the experience of CinCHouse, a long absence does not make the heart grow fonder—it makes it resentful of having to be alone and raise children as a single parent. Do not agree to an unaccompanied tour unless there is absolutely no choice. If necessary, look for civilian accommodations to keep you and your family close to your service member. You would be surprised at how many "unaccompanied" service members are joined by their spouses in Japan, Korea, and elsewhere.

Generally speaking, the military prefers to intersperse popular duty stations with less-popular ones. The value of a duty station is determined subjectively by the location as well as the frequency of deployment or hardship. So, for example, a one-year unaccompanied Army supply tour in Afghanistan could be considered as bad as an accompanied, nondeploying three-year tour in South Korea. By contrast, a post at Lakenheath

Air Force Base (**AFB**) in England might be considered as terrific as a post near grandparents in San Antonio, Texas.

Another factor in relocation is that the military tends to relocate families within regions because it is costly to move households across the country or around the world. Thus, West Coast–based families are likely to stay on the West Coast or move to the Pacific Rim (such as Hawaii or Japan), but they are not likely to get stationed in Europe. Occasionally they relocate from the West Coast to the East Coast or vice versa. East Coast–based families are likely to relocate to Europe or to the West Coast, but not to the Pacific Rim.

—— Did You Know? ——

Service members who request an unaccompanied tour unknowingly send up a red flag to their superiors. Such a request is usually an indication of family problems that the service member is trying to avoid. More often than not, the service member uses the lengthy separation as an excuse to get a divorce.

Knowing these factors allows you to take control of your family's destiny by plotting out your goals for future duty stations. They may seem confusing, so here are some examples:

Sarah and Ben

Sarah works in Washington, D.C., where her husband, Ben, is stationed at the Pentagon as a submarine warfare specialist. Although she loves her job, she dreams of living in Europe someday. The couple has also agreed that they want Sarah to stay home when they raise a family, and Ben would like to live close to his parents in Florida and not have to spend too much time away from his growing kids.

Because the couple already lives on the East Coast, and a political desk job at the Pentagon is not considered to be a popular billet compared to being out in the field, Ben is able to work with his detailer to go on an exchange program in London with the Royal Navy for two years—

fulfilling Sarah's dream. Upon return, however, he is required to go to a deploying submarine billet, but he is able to find something in unpopular Kings Bay, Georgia, which is 30 minutes from his parents in Jacksonville, Florida. With his experience in the submarine community, Ben knows that "Boomers" (the big submarines carrying nuclear weapons) deploy for less duration than fast-attack submarines, and he is able to get himself assigned to a Boomer. Although Sarah has difficulty finding a job in Kings Bay, the cost of living is very inexpensive and she sees Ben enough that they can easily start a family while she stays home.

Debbie and Steve

Debbie and Steve live in San Antonio with teenage children. At this stage of their lives, they do not wish to relocate because Debbie is at the top of her career as a corporate executive and they want to keep the children in the same school. Steve is currently an instructor at a tech school, but his branch manager says his next post will be tougher. Steve opts for an aviation job based in San Antonio, even though it means he deploys frequently for a total of six months per year throughout the three-year duration. After any deployment, he always comes back to home base in San Antonio.

Mindy and Evan

Evan just completed Marine Corps boot camp, but he knows he doesn't want to stay in the military forever, and neither does his fiancée, Mindy. In fact, he was enticed by the educational opportunities touted by the recruiter because he can't afford to go to college. Evan opted to get his technical training at a computer programming center, which happened to be in San Diego, where Mindy lives with her parents. Although he sometimes gets sent on difficult war games in the California desert for weeks at a time, his growing computer skills make him increasingly invaluable.

Not only does he get the opportunity to remain for a tour of duty at Camp Pendleton in San Diego, he is promoted early, and the additional pay allows him to get married sooner than he expected. However, Evan knows the second tour might mean deployment. As an alternative, he is considering going to a local university (paid for via the military's Montgomery G.I. Bill scholarship) or getting out and earning a $65,000 salary with a local software company.

Reservists' Duties

The recruiting brochure for Reservists says they typically drill one weekend out of every month and two weeks in the summertime. In reality, that schedule can change depending on the needs of the military and, to a lesser degree, how much extra time your family wants to schedule him for duty. My girlfriend Casey typically drills three days per weekend and spent 22 days on deployment last year—with only a few weeks' advance notice. So don't get the common mistaken impression that your hubby is just playing G.I. Joe for the weekends only! Your hubby may have the same misconception because he's in it for the extra pay and education benefits. Prepare yourself emotionally, logistically, and financially for the prospect of his being activated and deployed.

Reservist jobs are almost as diverse as those for active duty, so it's just as important to review a career track for potential downsides. In particular, some Reservists such as medical personnel are far more likely to be activated and deployed than others. Ask your service member's colleagues about their experiences and what is likely to occur.

WAR STORIES

When Training Feels Like Deployment

When my husband and I were stationed at the Marine Corps' Camp Pendleton, we noticed that the service members seemed to be gone all the time. We discovered that the Marine infantry units frequently train in the nearby desert base of Twentynine Palms (jokingly referred to as "29 Stumps"). Most infantrymen on shore duty spent two weeks out of the month in training, making shore duty sometimes feel as bad as sea duty—but without the extra pay.

Differences Between Military and Civilian Jobs

As you can see, there are tremendous benefits to a military career, just as there are hurdles to overcome. Comparisons to civilian careers are difficult, and you cannot factor in the costs of relocation and deployment. Although military service members are paid 4 to 10 percent less than their civilian counterparts—and wives often have difficulty maintaining an income because of frequent relocations to unusual areas—how many companies do you know that offer free education, amazing benefits, and the opportunity to live in dream locations such as Europe? Your hubby may also like the military because of the excitement and mission. After all, how many cooks or nurses get to brag to their friends about target practice with an M16 or flying in an Apache helicopter? Finally, your kids will appreciate the closely knit community that will greet them anywhere in the world.

Did You Know?

A revoked security clearance could end a service member's career. Yet the leading reason for revoked clearances is personal financial problems! That's because creditors know and frequently do call up a debtor's commanding officer and demand that he pay up. Doing so is technically illegal, but it never fails to work. When the commanding officer hears about a service member's mounting debt and his wife's uncontrollable shopping sprees, he will insist that the service member pay and probably require him to participate in financial counseling. Regardless, the situation immediately sends up a red flag and threatens the service member's status. So be sure to pay your bills on time and lay off the trips to the mall!

Unlike civilian companies, the military will get involved in your personal life, for good or bad. Because the military community lives and works together, because military families are de facto diplomats overseas, and because personal issues can affect national security, the military simply has no choice but to acknowledge and regulate the personal lives of its service members.

Spousal and child abuse, for example, can end a service member's career, and neighbors *will* call his command to report it—as they should. You don't find that kind of protection in civilian neighborhoods these days! Military families also have been on the watch for post-traumatic stress disorder (**PTSD**) among combat veterans. PTSD affects approximately 30 percent of deployed service members and can result in debilitating mental health problems and abuse. On the downside, extreme personal financial problems can cause your hubby to lose his security clearance because of the increased risk of bribery.

Finally, the biggest difference between military and civilian life is that the "boss" provides more comprehensive support for the families of the "employee." You will find help around every corner to get you through relocation, career changes, child care, and all kinds of household issues, because the military understands that a service member's morale—and therefore his decision to remain in the service—are often determined by the stability of the family supporting him.

The Least You Need to Know

> If you understand how your service member's career track works and what he is destined for, you can better control your family's destiny in terms of your relocations, your job stability, and how frequently he deploys.
> Some form of training kicks off every service member's career. It's a brutal separation, but it's important to let your man get through it without nagging him, so you can move on to better times.
> Try to learn as much as possible about a career track or command before your service member takes a position with it. His colleagues can tell you how much he is likely to relocate and deploy, and give you the unofficial scoop on what life will really be like.
> You will have to relocate at some point. The key is learning what options you have and working the system to get what's right for you. You

and your service member will need to discuss your dream and make a ten-year plan.

RESOURCES

Please note that these websites seem to change their URLs constantly, but the service remains the same.

> www.staynavy.navy.mil—A career development website for sailors.
> sso.mol.usmc.mil/SSO—A career development site for Marines.
> www.marinenet.usmc.mil/marinenet/—A Marine Corps portal for classes and career advancement.
> www.us.army.mil—Army Knowledge Online is a career development and information site for the Army.
> www.my.af.mil—An Air Force online portal for classes and career advancement.
> If you want to do research on career tracks anonymously, check out the official website of your military service or talk to a recruiter. Also, visit Internet discussion groups of service members in career tracks and ask them about their jobs.

CHAPTER 4

Community *and* Family Resources

Government and Nonprofit Organizations

Just when you thought you had to face military life alone, be assured that help is always available. In fact, there is a wide variety of family support organizations out there, both government-run and nonprofit groups. Their job is to help you cope with the rougher aspects of military life. The government offices in particular know "when Mama ain't happy, ain't nobody happy," meaning that an unhappy family will ultimately drive a service member out of the military and begin to harm retention levels.

To begin with, there are a number of new-spouse orientation programs offered by a variety of organizations, depending on which base you live at. Most Marine Corps bases, for example, offer the highly recommended **L.I.N.K.S.** program. The Navy's version is **COMPASS**, and the Army has Army Family Team Building, or **AFTB**. These amazing programs will get you up to speed in a hurry, and you'll find some good friends and counselors. Ask around and check your base newspaper to find out which orientation programs are most helpful.

The government-sponsored family support offices can also be a terrific resource. In typical bureaucratic fashion, they are given different names by different services, so it might also be called the Family Services Center or Family Support Center (**FSC**), Fleet & Family Support Center (**FFSC**), Marine Corps Community Services (**MCCS**), or Army Community Services (**ACS**). For practical purposes, this book will simply refer to the Family Support Center, or FSC. Additionally, the Department of Defense created MilitaryOneSource, which conveniently provides services via a website (militaryonesource.com) and a 1-800 number.

The FSC on your base is staffed with a dozen or so counselors to assist you in dealing with such critical issues as career resources and training opportunities for spouses, relocation assistance, and personal financial counseling. More recently, career training and job placement have been expanded to include licensing programs. Several military services also have teamed up with job placement agencies to provide spouses with job benefits and training in addition to job placement as the spouse relocates.

Did You Know?

Occupational licenses, such as for nursing, obtained in one state may not be valid in another state. This is particularly true in California. Check with the career counselor or state occupational safety board website to find out if your occupational license is accepted at your new duty station.

Relocation assistance is probably the biggest reason why you will use the FSC. The counselor can personally walk you through a move, especially a complicated overseas move, and provide you with brochures and contacts on your new base. This information also can be found at Military HOMEfront site www.militaryinstallations.dod.mil.

Equally important, the relocation counselor is your cash king! He or she can help you determine how much extra money you will receive to cover the cost of the move and whether a "do it yourself" (**DITY**) move would be more or less costly than allowing a professional company to handle your move at the military's expense.

FSC is also home to Family Advocacy, the agency responsible for handling domestic violence cases among military families. Family advocates are not perfect human beings, but when contacted promptly with all the information, they do a great job representing abused spouses, sometimes in the face of a service member backed by a command full of men. Indeed, it is important to remember that the military is responsible for its employees, i.e., service members, and not their families. The minute some military supervisors begin to see a family break up, they assume the spouse should be cut off from key services, such as access to legal and financial support, to protect the interests of the service member. Know your rights, girlfriend! Family advocates understand this process, which is reasonable, and know how to work the system on behalf of the spouse. Domestic abuse will also be discussed later, in chapter 13, "Preventing Trouble in Paradise."

Did You Know?

The Military HOMEfront websites contain the same information as the brochure handed to you by the relocation counselor. The best information at Military HOMEfront is not the description of your new base but the telephone numbers and e-mail addresses for resources there. Armed with e-mail addresses, you can start to communicate with critical contacts such as the housing office.

MilitaryOneSource has all these resources and more, including arranging six free mental health counseling sessions for military families upon request and total anonymity whenever services are provided. In fact, MilitaryOneSource can handle just about any request, including finding child care and real estate resources.

Finally, the FSC is home to key financial support services within the Army and Air Force: the Army Emergency Relief and Air Force Aid Society. In the Navy and Marine Corps, these services are provided by a nonprofit organization known as the Navy–Marine Corps Relief Society (**NMCRS**). Basically, these organizations provide emergency financial support to military families in need. For example, if a bureaucratic glitch causes your military pay to be delayed, these organizations can immediately advance you the amount if you agree to pay them back upon receipt of the delayed funds. They also provide interest-free loans for things such as car repairs, emergency trips home, and some medical services not covered by Tricare. Really extraordinary expenses are covered by grants that do not need to be repaid.

What's the catch? These organizations want you to take responsibility for and control of your personal finances, and they will help you do that not only through emergency funding but also through budget counseling. Typically, a financial counselor will start by reviewing your monthly income and expenses and then discuss your immediate financial needs. If you don't show responsibility for your personal finances, they won't provide emergency funds—and can you blame them?

In addition to providing emergency funds, these organizations are terrific resources to help you figure out your household income and ex-

WAR STORIES

Could I Be Paid Now, Please?

For months, my husband (a Navy diver stationed at the Experimental Dive Unit) came home proudly telling me how he had earned an extra $150 in Hazardous Duty Pay that month by diving to extreme depths as part of a human guinea pig experiment his department was running. Each month we would gleefully put an extra $150 on our credit cards with dinners at Sonny's Barbeque Pit and shopping sprees at Baby Gap. Neither of us checked to see if my husband had actually been paid, and sure enough, three months and $450 in debt later, I discovered we had not. Someone had forgotten to enter the Hazardous Duty Pay in the system. My husband corrected the problem and we were reimbursed the entire amount, but not for another month. And we had to pay off the credit card interest that had accrued over four months.

penses in preparation for major changes in your life. For example, it's a great idea to visit a budget counselor when you're anticipating a promotion, relocation, divorce, or new baby. A budget counselor can help you determine exactly how much money you will earn and what your expenditures will be so you can be prepared and plan ahead. The NMCRS "Budget for Baby" class is especially famous for its good advice on financial preparations for a new baby as well as guidance on what items new parents will need and how to get them cheaply. Of course, class participants also appreciate the fantastic "Baby Sea Bag" full of handmade blankets and other goodies they walk away with.

Speaking of babies, there are Child Development Centers (**CDC**) on most bases that give steep discounts on day care. The CDC also provides 24-hour care for those service members who have night duty. There's usually a long waiting list, but single service members and dual-military couples get priority. The CDC also offers home day care certification for military wives who want to open day care businesses in their homes, so check out that option, too.

Civil Servants vs. Bureaucrats: How to Get Business Done on Base

Be forewarned: All of these organizations, both government and non-profit, *can* be plagued by bureaucrats. Although the dictionary may not distinguish between a civil servant and a bureaucrat, anyone who has dealt with both will notice an immediate difference. Civil servants are those angels who genuinely care about helping military families. They always go above and beyond the call of duty to make sure you're taken care of. Do not abuse these people by pushing them too hard, or they will turn into bureaucrats. Bureaucrats are employees who couldn't care less about your problems, even if it is their job to care.

I raise this issue to help you get your business done with these often difficult people. The favorite word of a bureaucrat is "no." Why? Because "no" is a very powerful word that often forces you to beg for their help. Also, the word "no" prevents them from actually having to work.

The key is to prepare yourself for obstacles in advance, be armed with a pen to fill out countless forms, and always behave calmly and professionally. Never, ever yell at or insult a bureaucrat, no matter how obnoxious he or she may be. If a bureaucrat poses an apparently insurmountable obstacle, you always have two options. First, ask him or her, "What do you think the solution to this problem is?" This forces the bureaucrat to articulate your options. Never say, "Do you think I can get this done?" The automatic answer to that question is "no"—and that is not the answer you want.

Did You Know?

Cha-ching! Although some families can actually make money on relocation by cutting costs, most families lose an average of $800 per move, according to recent statistics. In chapter 9 you will see tips and tricks for making a move, but suffice it to say that it's a good idea to meet with a relocation counselor at the FSC or personnel office for your first relocation.

Your second option is to go through the chain of command to the supervisor. This is really the better option if a bureaucrat is unwilling to help you. However, this will be effective only if you have remained calm and professional throughout your discussion with the bureaucrat. This is where yelling or insulting the bureaucrat really harms you, because no supervisor will want to go near a crazed military wife. But if you've behaved calmly and professionally, the supervisor will feel bad for how poorly you've been treated and will go the extra mile to solve your problem. Better yet, you may be doing everyone a service by effectively notifying the supervisor of your poor treatment by his or her employees and putting the bureaucrat on report. The next time the bureaucrat deals with a wife or female service member, the bureaucrat will be on his or her best behavior!

WAR STORIES

Why Not?

When I really get ticked off by a stonewalling bureaucrat, my favorite response is "Why not?" It is a wonderfully generic response to the word "no" that forces the bureaucrat to explain further. "Are you sure?" is another fun retort because it challenges the bureaucrat to look for more information.

These responses came in handy when I went to sign up for surfing lessons with Kahuna Bob at Camp Pendleton early one summer. When I asked the young woman at the beach shack about it, she immediately responded that they did not offer surfing lessons. "Why not?" I said. "You did last year." "No, we didn't," the woman responded with perfect confidence. After a few rallies of "Yes, you did" and "No, we didn't," I asked, "Are you sure?" The woman acknowledged that she was not sure since it was her first week on the job. She was sure, however, that they would never offer a class like that. "Why not?" I asked. Exasperated, the woman got off her duff and found her boss, who handed her the sign-up sheet for the next week's surfing class.

Spouse Clubs and Command Family Support Groups

If official family support organizations are there to provide you with vital information, spouse clubs and Family Readiness Groups (**FRG**s) are there to be your friends and compadres. These are women who walk in the same shoes and know what you are going through. They are there for you in the middle of the night when the baby is screaming and your husband is off playing G.I. Joe in a faraway land. Ignore your silly hubby and his friends if they tell you these groups are nothing but gossipy henhouses. They don't know what they're talking about, and they will have no solutions for you when you ask where to find new friends or babysitters while they are gone. In fact, this is one area where you are fully authorized as CinCHouse to tell them to shut their traps.

Spouse clubs are typically organizations of military spouses on your base or in your command. Usually there is a club for spouses of enlisted men's wives and one for officers' wives, although bases and commands are increasingly integrating their spouse clubs to share mutual interests as well as to increase participation.

In the old days, the spouse clubs were your sources for information on where your husband was and what he might be doing, but they also would keep anxious families busy with long luncheons and hours of bingo. Today's spouse clubs increasingly cater to working wives, with evening events and Web-based newsletters that can update you at your office. Good clubs also offer child care during meetings. Most important, this is your opportunity to quickly meet other wives who share common interests. Spouse clubs reinforce these friendships by organizing social events for the whole family and opportunities for extensive volunteer work on base. The adage that "friendships are experiences shared" holds true with spouse clubs, and you'll meet lifelong friends whom you'll later visit around the world throughout your military career.

Family Readiness Groups, sometimes referred to as command spouse clubs, also socialize frequently, but their primary purpose is to provide information on the status of a deployed command, offer counseling and support to troubled families, and keep families busy and focused on positive things such as preparing a spectacular homecoming party for their command. They are run by elected leaders, not necessarily the wife of the commanding officer. Whether led by the commanding officer's wife or not, these leaders stay closely connected with the command higher-ups, especially during deployments, and are your connection if something goes terribly wrong with your family.

Additionally, your command has volunteer wives you can turn to in an emergency, particularly during a deployment. These are known as **Ombudsmen** in the Navy and Army and **Key Volunteers** in the Marine Corps. If you have to go to the emergency room while your hubby is deployed, these are the women who will quickly arrange babysitting for your kids—so be nice and support them whenever possible.

Perhaps the best thing about family support groups is that, once again, these are women who walk in your shoes and are going through the same things you are—so go to these meetings! Don't ignore your fellow wives or think you're better than they are for being more independent. You will regret this thinking within one month of your husband's deployment, when you're all alone with no one to talk to.

And spouse clubs and family support groups are fun! The first meeting is always difficult because you are meeting new people, but you'll feel better knowing that they are normal people just like you. By the third meeting you'll be hooking up with friends for lunch and other activities outside the spouse club.

What Are Other Military Wives and Female Service Members Like, Anyway?

My first introduction to other military wives occurred when my girlfriend MaryAnn held the first party for our new command. At the time, I was a high-powered public relations executive working in downtown Washington, D.C., and I was absolutely certain the other wives would be far beneath me. MaryAnn could not have been nicer, which only reaffirmed my prejudice. She inquired about my work, my hobbies, and whether I had kids, always genuinely interested in what I had to say. She then suggested getting together for lunch with some of the other wives. I reluctantly agreed, but only because she had thrown a heck of a party and I appreciated the opportunity to meet other spouses, half of whom were also working women in interesting jobs.

My second encounter with MaryAnn embarrasses me to this day. After yapping long enough about myself, I finally asked about her adventures in military life and what I could expect. It turned out that Mary-Ann, who was married to an F-14 backseater, had lived all over the world. In fact, two days after getting married, she had moved to Tokyo and been left by her deploying husband to find an apartment, a car, a job, and a life. MaryAnn told fascinating stories about escorting her husband's aircraft carrier to port in Thailand in a speedboat full of bikini-clad, whooping wives excited to see their husbands. She has entertained diplomats and foreign military service members in just about all types of occasions all over the world.

──────────── *Did You Know?* ────────────

Opening a day care center in your home is incredibly profitable while allowing you to stay home! Day care is scarce on many bases, and families are willing to pay up to $300 per child per week in some locations. That's $1,200 per month—and you can earn more by caring for more children! The CDC will train you, and the relief organizations can lend you money to pay for insurance up front.

The bottom line was that I was greatly mistaken for thinking Mary-Ann was some naive little military wife with nothing else to do. She was simply reaching out to me because she understood the importance of quickly establishing friendships. Life and duty stations are too short for the kind of condescension I first showed MaryAnn, and I thank my lucky stars she persisted in making friends because I would have been terribly lonely without her.

MaryAnn is a good example of the friendliness you'll see in other military wives, so don't mistake it as their being naive or silly. But friendliness is not the only familiar characteristic of military wives. Most military wives are career women. In fact, DoD surveys show that 91 percent of junior enlisted spouses (pay grades E-1 to E-5) work and 74 percent of all spouses are employed outside the home, while only 57 percent of civilian women work. As noted before, this is a tremendous change from the old stereotype of the World War II–era wives hanging laundry and pining away for their deployed husbands.

Military families also tend to be young, marry young, and have young children at home. Forty-seven percent of service members have children, and 73 percent are under age nine. By contrast, only 32 percent of civilian families have children at all.

Despite our youth, the typical military family is better educated and more comfortable with technology than the average American. In fact, 92.8 percent of military families report having access to the Internet, compared to only 50 percent of civilians. This can be partly attributed to the fact that the Internet has become the primary way for military families to keep in touch with a deployed service member. As one recent DoD study states, "On the whole, military spouses are highly educated, with 97 percent having completed at least a high school education, compared to 84 percent of all adults 25 years or older in the nation (Census Bureau, 2005). The typical spouse of enlisted members had at least some college experience, whereas the typical spouse of an officer had a four-year degree. The majority of spouses indicated furthering their education was a goal (78 to 95 percent).

Finally, the military is one of the most racially diverse institutions in the nation. Approximately 19 percent of service members and their families are African American, compared to the national average of 12 percent, and 4 percent indicated themselves as being "more than one race."

Keep these statistics in mind when you meet other military wives for the first time. Above all, forget the stereotypes. Military wives are smart, educated, career- and family-oriented folks like you. And they're definitely people worth getting to know!

The Case for Getting Involved

So you've just moved (again), you've gotten the family settled, and, well, it's lonely. It's time to start building a community around you and your family.

"Where to start?" so many women ask. It's not as easy anymore without the "insta-community" wives used to have available in the form of spouse clubs. Spouse club membership has declined for many reasons, both good and bad.

One of the worst reasons for the decline of spouse clubs these days is that no one wants to be a "joiner." The cultural phenomenon of everyone stressing their independence and self-sufficiency contrasts directly with the need to build communities of people with common interests.

We as military wives and women in uniform need to ask ourselves:

Is this a healthy attitude for me and my family, given that we will relocate every three years and given that relocation tops the "most stressful" lists? Not only will you benefit personally, but also by building a network around yourself, you can help your husband and kids become acquainted with new friends. Everyone knows the benefits of having friends around to support you in difficult times. The question is how to go about it.

Spouse clubs are the most obvious places to begin building a community, because they focus on a common interest: women living on and/or recently moving to a military base. However, there are many other types of organizations that may pique your interest. Consider looking into the following opportunities:

> Book clubs
> Philanthropic and assistance organizations, such as Army Family Team Building, Key Volunteers, the Navy–Marine Corps Relief Society, and other nonprofit organizations on base
> Fitness clubs or tennis, golf, hiking, biking, and SCUBA diving
> Women's networking groups such as the local women's chamber of commerce or local professional organizations
> Kids' play groups (Gymboree has classes for babies as young as three months)
> Local government recreational offerings such as writing workshops and art classes
> Investment and finance clubs
> Churches or other houses of worship
> College or continuing education courses

Check your local newspaper, library, or bookstore for notices of upcoming meetings.

What if you go to a meeting and don't like what's going on? All the more reason to get involved! You're probably not the only one who thinks things could be better, and if you don't change things, who will? There are lots of ways to change the direction of family organizations on base. Become a command family leader such as an Ombudsman or Key Volunteer. Volunteer your services at nonprofit organizations such as Fisher

Cheap Vacations

Before they had kids, my girlfriend MaryAnn and her husband were always going on vacation to places such as Las Vegas, the North Carolina beaches, and Europe. She also seemed to have frequent houseguests of old friends who wanted to take their kids to visit Washington, D.C., where MaryAnn lived. When I asked her how the couple could afford so many vacations, she explained that they simply stayed with friends they had met at different duty stations over the years, especially through the spouse clubs. MaryAnn kept in touch by e-mail and Christmas cards over the years, and the friends gladly exchanged visits as a way to vacation inexpensively while catching up.

House or the base thrift store. Or even organize base groups over the Web through support sites such as CinCHouse.com.

Finally, remember what it's like to move to a new base. Introduce yourself to new neighbors and support community organizations. Your good deed may come back to help you someday.

The Least You Need to Know

> There are resources available to help you in every emergency imaginable. The Family Support Center is your first stop.
> There are two kinds of government employees—civil servants and bureaucrats—but you need to be nice to both and learn how to negotiate to get things done.
> Spouse clubs and family readiness groups are terrific resources for you to meet new friends and get through stressful times together, particularly when the command goes on deployment.
> Getting involved in your community helps you and your family get settled as soon as possible and eases the stress of relocating.

> Other military wives are just like you! So give them a chance and get to know them.

RESOURCES

> www.militaryinstallations.dod.mil—Military HOMEfront is a critical website to get official orientation packets for any military base online. Watch out! This is official propaganda, so you will still need to research the unofficial scoop on any base to find out the bad stuff.
> www.cinchouse.com—Check out the discussion forums and the list of spouse groups in the Hubs who host their websites with CinCHouse.

CHAPTER 5

Protocol, *or* How *to* Get Along *in a* Hierarchy

Ranks and Privileges

Most civilians think the military hierarchy is either cool or totally outdated. Either way, it seems very foreign. Certainly, very few employers these days give promotions according to the number of years of service (as opposed to pure merit) and then incorporate that hierarchy into the social structure.

Because the military is so closely knit, you hang out together as much as you work together. Even in today's world, and despite what others may tell you, socializing is helpful to your service member's career—not to mention the fact that it's important for quickly meeting new friends and establishing your family in a community. Service members who mingle are seen as good for improving morale among fellow service members and their families. These social butterflies and their wives get to know their superiors and stand out in a crowd at promotion time.

Spouses who support their service members' efforts to socialize are even more of an asset. I'm not talking about the demure Miss Melly, who holds back her opinions; I'm talking about normal, friendly people getting together for fun and conversation. Command officials often view such spouses as real assets in providing friendship and leadership to other families in the command. This is all very unofficial, of course, and no command is legally permitted to insist that you participate, but this is one of the great unspoken rules for success in the military.

Did You Know?

Command spouse clubs and family readiness groups have traditionally been led by the commanding officer's wife. Since even COs' wives frequently have full-time jobs and don't have time for such duties, more junior wives have taken advantage of the opportunity to step into that role. As a result, they get to meet with the CO and other command leaders at least monthly and socialize even more often. And that kind of leadership certainly reflects well on their husbands.

The military hierarchy does come into play during social occasions. Most important, know that there are rules prohibiting "fraternization" between officers and enlisted service members and, to some degree, between junior and senior ranks. What fraternization means exactly can be up for interpretation, but it basically means that officers and senior enlisted are supposed to keep a professional distance from the junior service members they supervise. Getting drunk with your subordinates is definitely off-limits, but other situations are less clear, especially since these rules do not apply to family members. Can you party hearty at an off-base neighborhood block party that includes people from different ranks? If you are close friends with the spouse of someone from the opposite rank, can you invite her husband over for dinner? All I can say is that you have to decide on a case-by-case basis.

The consequences of fraternization are also unclear. While there is no specific punishment we have heard of, we are aware that fraternization can lead to decreased respect and increased resentment in the workplace—and that can harm the career of your service member. For example, if you are the wife of a junior enlisted service member and become best friends with the commanding officer's wife, other families may think your service member's recent promotion was the result of favoritism. Or the commanding officer may feel he has to go out of his way to prevent the appearance of favoritism by adding burdensome duties on your service member. The military does not want enlisted service members to become too close to an officer and begin to question or laugh off the officer's authority. There is no room in combat for a democracy, and the hierarchy is there to ensure that orders are swiftly given and acted upon for the safety of the entire unit.

For all these reasons, spouses need to understand what the pecking order is, generally speaking, and what the appropriate protocol is.

Did You Know?

If a service member cheats on his wife with another service member in their command, he could get into big trouble for fraternization. Commanding officers have lost their rank and been kicked out of the military for conviction on this charge, so take it seriously and know your resources in case a husband strays.

What the Uniform Means

Whether you know it or not, your service member wears his résumé on his chest. Ribbons, medals, or pieces of tin (or lack thereof) synopsize his service in the military or identify his rank. When your service member sees another service member, he initiates or responds to a salute according to the rank on the other. You do not need to know all the ribbons and ranks—and you will never salute anyone!—but you do need to understand the chain of command and the basic symbols that represent each level.

Please note that there is a difference between a **rank**, such as "captain," and a **pay grade**, ranging from E-1 to E-9 for enlisted, O-1 to O-10 for officers, and W-1 to W-5 for warrant officers. Further, different services have different ranks at different pay grades. Thus an Army captain is in a midranking pay grade of O-3, but a Navy captain is a big-shot O-6!

Following are detailed pictures of rank insignia from the Department of Defense (DoD). Rank insignia are generally seen on the shirt collars, shoulders, or sleeves of the uniform. Although these look complex, all you really need to notice is whether the person is wearing a chevron or "stripes" (meaning he is enlisted), metallic bars (a junior officer or war-rant officer), oak-leaf clusters (a midlevel officer), or eagles or stars (a senior officer). Once you visualize these images, you'll notice that some service members have more stripes or different bars than others. The more stripes they have, the higher-ranking they are. And among bars or oak leaves, silver is higher-ranking than its gold counterpart.

Other uniform items, such as a stripe on the pant leg, which identi-fies some enlisted ranks, can help you navigate the hierarchy. However, the rank insignia is what your service member is looking for when he approaches another service member and determines whether to initiate a salute to a higher rank or respond to a salute from a lower-ranking service member.

Officer Rank Insignia

Officer ranks in the U.S. military consist of commissioned officers and warrant officers. The commissioned ranks are the highest in the mili-tary. These officers hold presidential commissions and are confirmed at their ranks by the Senate. Army, Air Force, and Marine Corps officers are called company-grade officers in the pay grades of O-1 to O-3, field-grade officers in pay grades O-4 to O-6, and general officers in pay grades O-7 and higher. The equivalent officer groupings in the Navy are called junior grade, midgrade, and flag.

Warrant officers hold warrants from their service secretary and are specialists or experts in certain military technologies or capabilities. The lowest-ranking warrant officers serve under a warrant, but they receive commissions from the president upon promotion to chief warrant offi-cer 2. These commissioned warrant officers are direct representatives of the president of the United States. They derive their authority from the same source as commissioned officers but remain specialists, in contrast

COMMISSIONED

	ARMY	AIR FORCE	NAVY	MARINE CORPS	COAST GUARD
SPECIAL	GENERAL OF THE ARMY (GA)		FLEET ADMIRAL (FADM)		
O-10	GENERAL (GEN)	GENERAL (Gen)	ADMIRAL (ADM)	GENERAL (Gen)	ADMIRAL (ADM)
O-9	LIEUTENANT GENERAL (LTG)	LIEUTENANT GENERAL (Lt Gen)	VICE ADMIRAL (VADM)	LIEUTENANT GENERAL (LtGen)	VICE ADMIRAL (VADM)
O-8	MAJOR GENERAL (MG)	MAJOR GENERAL (Maj Gen)	REAR ADMIRAL (RADM)	MAJOR GENERAL (MajGen)	REAR ADMIRAL (RADM)
O-7	BRIGADIER GENERAL (BG)	BRIGADIER GENERAL (Brig Gen)	REAR ADMIRAL LOWER (RADML)	BRIGADIER GENERAL (BGen)	REAR ADMIRAL LOWER (RADML)
O-6	COLONEL (COL)	COLONEL (Col)	CAPTAIN (CAPT)	COLONEL (Col)	CAPTAIN (CAPT)
O-5	LIEUTENANT COLONEL (LTC)	LIEUTENANT COLONEL (Lt Col)	COMMANDER (CDR)	LIEUTENANT COLONEL (LtCol)	COMMANDER (CDR)

to commissioned officers, who are generalists. There are no warrant officers in the Air Force.

Naval officers wear distinctively different rank devices depending on the uniform they're wearing. The three basic uniforms and rank devices used are: khakis, collar insignia pins; whites, stripes on shoulder boards; and blues, stripes sewn on the lower coat sleeves.

Source: The Department of Defense Almanac.

Enlisted Rank Insignia

Service members in pay grades E-1 through E-3 are usually either in some kind of training status or on their initial assignment. The training includes the basic training phase, where recruits are immersed in military culture and values and are taught the core skills required by their service component.

Basic training is followed by a specialized or advanced training phase that provides recruits with a specific area of expertise or concentration. In the Army and Marines this area is called a military occupational specialty; in the Navy it is known as a rate; and in the Air Force it is simply called an Air Force specialty.

ENLISTED

	ARMY	AIR FORCE	NAVY	MARINE CORPS	COAST GUARD	
	STAFF SERGEANT (SSG)	TECH SERGEANT E-6 (TSgt)	PETTY OFFICER 1ST CLASS (PO1)	STAFF SERGEANT (SSgt)	PETTY OFFICER 1ST CLASS (PO1)	E-6
	SERGEANT (SGT)	STAFF SERGEANT E-5 (SSgt)	PETTY OFFICER 2ND CLASS (PO2)	SERGEANT (Sgt)	PETTY OFFICER 2ND CLASS (PO2)	E-5
	CORPORAL (CPL) SPECIALIST (SPC)	SENIOR AIRMAN E-4 (SrA)	PETTY OFFICER 3RD CLASS (PO3)	CORPORAL (Cpl)	PETTY OFFICER 3RD CLASS (PO3)	E-4
	PRIVATE FIRST CLASS (PFC)	AIRMAN 1ST CLASS E-3 (A1C)	SEAMAN (SN)	LANCE CORPORAL (Lcpl)	SEAMAN (SN)	E-3
	PRIVATE E-2 (PV2)	AIRMAN E-2 (AMN)	SEAMAN APPRENTICE (SA)	PRIVATE 1ST CLASS (PFC)	SEAMAN APPRENTICE (SA)	E-2
	PRIVATE E-1 (PV1) NO INSIGNIA	AIRMAN BASIC E-1 (AB) NO INSIGNIA	SEAMAN RECRUIT (SR)	PRIVATE (Pvt) NO INSIGNIA	SEAMAN RECRUIT (SR)	E-1

© Copyright 2002 MOA Press

WARRANT

ARMY	NAVY	MC	COAST GUARD
WARRANT OFFICER 5 (CW5)		WARRANT OFFICER 5 (CWO5)	
WARRANT OFFICER 4 (CW4)	WARRANT OFFICER 4 (CWO4)	WARRANT OFFICER 4 (CWO4)	WARRANT OFFICER 4 (CWO4)
WARRANT OFFICER 3 (CW3)	WARRANT OFFICER 3 (CWO3)	WARRANT OFFICER 3 (CWO3)	WARRANT OFFICER 3 (CWO3)
WARRANT OFFICER 2 (CW2)	WARRANT OFFICER 2 (CWO2)	WARRANT OFFICER 2 (CWO2)	WARRANT OFFICER 2 (CWO2)
WARRANT OFFICER 1 (WO1)	WARRANT OFFICER 1 (CWO1)	WARRANT OFFICER 1 (CWO1)	

The U.S. Coast Guard is a part of the Department of Homeland Security in peacetime. Coast Guard rank insignia are the same as those for the Navy except for color and the seaman recruit rank, which has one stripe.

Leadership responsibility significantly increases in the midlevel enlisted ranks. This responsibility is given formal recognition by use of the terms "noncommissioned officer" and "petty officer." An Army sergeant, an Air Force staff sergeant, and a Marine corporal are considered NCO ranks. The Navy NCO equivalent, petty officer, is achieved at the rank of petty officer third class.

Sample Uniform Items

United States Army Class "A" Uniform
Quick Finder

Beret Flash

DUI
Distinctive Unit Insignia

Enlisted Branch/U.S.
Gold Lapel Disc

Regimental
Crest

Chevrons
for Class A
Uniform

Name
Plate

Beret

DUI
Distinctive Unit Insignia

Class A
Unit Patch

Service
Ribbon and
Holders

Qualification
Bars/Badges

Service
Stripes

Oxford
Shoes

Overseas Service
Stripes

Army Officer Garrison Cap

Beret (Enlisted)

Beret (Officer)

Blue Cap–Company Grade Officer

Blue Cap (Enlisted)

Blue Cap–Field Grade Officer

Blue Cap–General   **Blue Cap–Warrant Officer**

Medical Insignia

Officer   **Enlisted**

And Your Name Is . . . ?

Once you figure out the rank, you've solved one of the great battles of etiquette on the face of the planet: remembering the names of people you've been introduced to. Let me explain.

Let's say you are introduced to a Captain Ernie Buckforth. Thereafter, you would normally refer to him as "Captain Buckforth" or just plain "Captain." However, because most service members prefer that civilians call them by their first names during social occasions, Captain Buckforth will probably ask you to call him "Ernie." Thus, if you ever forget his

> ### WAR STORIES
>
> ## When Socializing Does Not Help His Career
>
> My girlfriend Joleen is normally very active with the submarine family support groups, but at her last command the spouse group was known for being gossipy troublemakers. Instead of associating herself with the spouse club, she and her friends did their own things to support the boat, including baking goodies for the office to enjoy and making take-out dinner runs for the guys on night duty. As she explains, it's best to use your own judgment as to whether your involvement will help or hurt.

name, simply greet him as "Captain"—which is signified on his rank—and wait for him to say, "Oh, please, call me Ernie."

You won't have as much luck with spouses, and really polite spouses can actually pose an etiquette problem, albeit a good one. My girlfriend Rose, for example, is the 30-year wife of the Command Master Chief (**CMC**) on a prominent aircraft carrier. That means her husband supervises all of 5,000 enlisted personnel on board, and he reports directly to the executive officer and commanding officer on their status. Rose, in her position, effectively takes leadership of the enlisted families whether or not she gets actively involved in the family support group. In her case, Rose advises younger, more enthusiastic wives to run the family support group and plays more of a background role.

The trouble with women like Rose is that they'll never introduce themselves as "Rose, wife of the CMC"—no decent and polite spouse would. She simply introduces herself as "Rose." Those spouses who know the CMC's last name might make the connection, but most spouses don't, and they go on to complain about the status of the enlisted on the ship. Rose says she likes to hear background info that she would not otherwise be told, but she has also heard several obnoxious spouses reveal highly sensitive information in undiplomatic terms (to say the least!). When Rose passes on the information to her husband, the spouse and

WAR STORIES

Not AT&T?

My girlfriend Belle tells a painful story about attending a very traditional tea hosted by the wife of a high-ranking Marine officer. As she walked in, the old dame held out a silver tray to a nervous young woman in front of Belle and asked for her calling card. The guest pulled out her AT&T card in front of the horrified hostess. Belle had to explain the faux pas: The hostess was expecting an old-fashioned calling card, which looks like a business card and provides her with your name so that she will know you attended, even if she does not get the chance to speak with you. Calling cards also allow hostesses to double-check your name and write thank-you notes if appropriate. Very few military wives these days use calling cards, but if you are asked for one, simply say that you have run out of them and not had a chance to go to the printer.

her service member aren't even aware that their unprofessional approach to complaining or revelation of sensitive information is being reported directly to the CMC!

The lesson here is always to behave professionally with other spouses and service members, because you never know who you're really talking to. Equally important, be polite about introducing yourself. Rose is the first to say that she did not earn her husband's rank—he did! So why would she introduce herself as the CMC's wife? And she doesn't want to have friends who are using her to advance their service members' careers.

What to Wear? The Appropriate Dress for Every Military Occasion

You will be invited to any number of different social events related to the military. These events are a blast if for no other reason than to see the military in its finest dress (you know you love those men in uniform!). Few lucky Army wives leave a "dining out" without being impressed by the Cavalry officers in traditional Stetson hats and riding boots. And those Navy whites will make you as giddy as you were the first time you watched Tom Cruise in *Top Gun*.

The most formal events include the annual service ball (such as the Army Birthday Ball) and diplomatic receptions, both of which can require formal ball gowns for spouses. The birthday balls are such a big occasion that groups of couples often rent hotel rooms for the night at the location of the event. Examples of slightly less formal events include a traditional "dining out," which is a command-sponsored dinner-and-dance party that includes spouses and girlfriends, and a Change of Command ceremony, which formally attaches and detaches command leadership to your unit. Finally, you will be invited to casual events such as command-sponsored picnics or promotion parties.

Did You Know?

A favorite activity of spouse clubs is to hold fashion shows in preparation for the service birthday ball. Club members parade the latest evening wear, meaning you get a sneak preview of what everyone else will be wearing at the ball. They will also tell you where the dress can be purchased and whether the retailer is offering a discount to military wives.

Military uniforms are confusing enough without trying to figure out the appropriate dress to wear when accompanying your service member. After all, the goal is to help your service member impress his colleagues and superiors with your classy clothes and good looks. Although trashy fashions are all the rage, anything that says "tramp" will make you a source of gossip. Trust me when I say the wife of the commanding officer will be commenting to her husband on everyone's dress as they drive home.

The first step is to check the invitation to see what is indicated or ask your man what he is wearing. If the invitation doesn't say, ask the hostess what she is wearing. On the following pages is a guide to help you through the quagmire.

Formal Ball

Military Dress

Army:	Navy:	Air Force:	Marines:
Dress Blues or Dress Mess; Class A uniforms may be appropriate if you do not have Dress Blues.	Mess Dress; whites or blues, depending on the season	Mess Dress	Dress Blue Bravos (with medals), Dress Blue Alphas (with ribbons and badges), or Service Alphas (green uniform)

Do
Formal gown; tuxedo for men. Be Cinderella for the evening!

Don't
Anything casual or so low-cut that your breasts fall out when you dance. Don't make yourself the subject of gossip at the watercooler on Monday.

Dining Out or Mess Night (a command-sponsored dinner with spouses)

Military Dress

Army:	Navy:	Air Force:	Marines:
Dress Blues or Mess; Class A uniforms may be appropriate if you do not have Dress Blues.	Dress Blues (winter) or formal "choker" whites (summer)	Service Dress or Mess Dress	Dress Blue Bravos (with medals), Dress Blue Alphas (with ribbons and badges), or Service Alphas (green uniform)

Do
Fancy cocktail dress or short formal gown; tuxedo or dark suit and tie for men

Don't
The suit you wore at the office that day or anything you might wear at a nightclub. "Church" dresses are also too innocent for the kind of fun you will have!

Change of Command, Hail and Farewell Party

Military Dress

Army:
Battle Dress Uniforms (BDUs) or "Duty Uniform"

Navy:
Service Dress Blues (winter) or formal "choker" whites (summer)

Air Force:
Fatigues or blues (uniform of the day)

Marines:
Dress Blue Deltas (brown shirt, blue pants) or Service Charlies (brown shirt, green pants)

Do
Evening: Evening dress—but no sequins. This is not the Academy Awards. Dark suit and tie for men.
Daytime: Floral dress or business suit unless the party is casual. Definitely ask the hostess.

Don't
Casual outfits, including jeans and bare midriffs, or anything your mother would not approve of.

Dinner at CO's House (or equivalent)

Military Dress

Ask the hostess. Usually civilian clothes: oxford shirt and slacks. Tie and jacket may be required.

Do
"Church clothes," such as floral dresses, nice slacks. Something you'd wear to a nice dinner with the in-laws.

Don't
Jeans or overly casual clothes (unless the hostess says okay); no bare midriffs or nose rings. Look responsible!

Command-Sponsored Picnic

Military Dress

Civilian clothes (polo shirt and shorts)

Do
Nice shorts and tennis shoes. If you expect to swim, limit your bathing suit exposure and bring a cover-up.

Don't
Miniskirts or other clothes that will inhibit your ability to play sports; absolutely no thong bikinis! This is not spring break!

(continued on next page)

Spouse Meetings

Do	Don't
Khaki pants and a casual top	If your mother would not approve, neither will the CO's wife.

Did You Know?

You are definitely not the only one who has difficulty remembering names. Particularly at large events, senior spouses often feel nervous and forget names—just like you. If you forget someone's name, the best thing to do is make everyone feel at home and joke about how forgetful you are, and ask her to say her name again. Repeat it three times, and then joke again about how you'll probably ask her ten more times. Most likely she has forgotten your name as well and will be grateful for the opportunity to ease the tension.

Socializing is a critical function of a spouse, even in the modern world. So get out there and have fun! Don't worry too much about protocol; it's far more important to be friendly and inviting. Not only are you helping your spouse's career, but also you may meet a few new friends.

The Least You Need to Know

- Expect to socialize with your service member's colleagues. Not only is it a great way to meet new friends, you're also helping him advance in his career.
- Be aware that officers and enlisted personnel are not allowed to "fraternize" with each other. They are required to keep a professional distance. This rule does not apply to family members.
- You can learn to distinguish who is who on base by learning more about rank insignia—the indications on your service member's clothing that spell out his rank and résumé.

❭ Dress appropriately for every occasion. Most important, don't dress like a tramp, or you will become the subject of watercooler gossip at your service member's office.

RESOURCE

❭ www.defenselink.mil/pubs/almanac/—The Department of Defense Almanac can explain in more detail the military hierarchy.

CHAPTER 6

Your Portable Career

As mentioned earlier, military wives and female service members are no longer the World War II–era sweethearts pining away at home. We are predominantly working women with goals and ambitions that extend way beyond taking care of our husbands. This is an important concept to understand because so many women underestimate the power their careers have in their lives. It's true that many spouses work to make ends meet, in part because the average service member earns about 4.5 percent less than his civilian counterpart. More important, however, career aspirations can be critical to the self-esteem of women today.

The working world cannot fulfill every emotional need of human beings, but there is no denying that some people need that daily sense of accomplishment and financial reward that only a career can provide. Military wives and female service members often do themselves an injustice by subordinating their professional needs and aspirations to the needs and desires of their husband and family. I'm not suggesting that all women should work; I just want you to be honest with yourself and find a balance that works for you and your family. Just remember, when Mama ain't happy, ain't nobody happy. So don't deprive yourself of emotional fulfillment from a career if you really need it. You'll be depriving your family of a happy wife and mother.

WAR STORIES

Online Networking with Fellow Wives

When Heather, who was stationed in Germany, found out her family had orders to move to California, she immediately jumped on the CinCHouse.com discussion boards to find out about her new base and meet new friends. In the process, she met another wife, Lisa, who was also a health care professional and learned that her license was not accepted by the state of California. But instead of suggesting that Heather reapply and take a licensing test, Lisa recommended that Heather apply for a job at the base hospital where she worked, since military health care facilities accept all state licenses. Before she had packed her bags in Germany, Heather had filled out an application and scheduled an interview.

I often see wives and female service members rob themselves of career fulfillment by accepting less-challenging positions or quitting work altogether. A recent survey of working spouses found that 42 percent felt that they were overqualified for the position they had accepted. The frequent relocation of military families, averaging one move every three years, adds to the burden of maintaining a spouse's career and is typically the excuse for blowing off career aspirations. A recent study by RAND, a prominent think tank, found that military wives earn as much as 60 percent less than their civilian counterparts, even though we tend to have higher education levels. Army and Air Force wives tend to fare worse than their Navy and Marine Corps counterparts. Why?

The answer lies in the frequency and place of relocation. In other words, it is difficult to maintain a career track when moving from Oklahoma City to Fort Benning, Georgia, to Japan in three-year stints. Navy wives have the easiest time because so many bases are in large port cities that offer significant job opportunities. For the other services, however, not only is it difficult to find a comparable job with comparable pay and skills, but spouses have the added burden of facing discrimination from

────────── *Did You Know?* ──────────

Elaine Neetz, employment readiness counselor at the FSC at Fort Wainwright, Alaska, writes:

When families determine that they are going to be relocating, working spouses looking for a job in the civil service should carry the following information with them to ensure that job hunting at the new location goes smoothly and employment is quicker and easier (depending on the job market, of course):

» Updated résumé and/or federal application (SF-171, OF-612)

» Professional certificates

» School transcripts

» At least three references (addresses, telephone numbers, points of contact)

» Awards, honors, letters of recommendation/appreciation, volunteer portfolio

» Federal employees should have Form SF-50 and Performance Appraisal or Form DD-214 if applying for the first time

» Recent work history

» Civilian employees should call their Civilian Personnel Office (CPO) for information about priority placement/extended leave without pay.

Most bases list their positions on their websites or at USAJOBS .gov with all the qualifying information that needs to be included. Spouses should consult with their local Family Support Center to inquire about the employment expert in their facility. This person should be able to assist any spouse in constructing the résumé to include all required CPO information. This information is usually on the CPO page at the installation's website.

employers who are tired of hiring employees who seem to relocate every time the wind changes. Further, many licensed professionals face the challenges of meeting different state standards, particularly California's, and having to reapply for a license every time they relocate. Finally, there is the issue of time and effort involved in quitting and finding a new job, often over long distances. Thus many spouses opt for low-paying, unchallenging positions or simply stop working altogether.

Do not despair! Your girlfriends at CinCHouse have several alternatives for those who want to continue their careers.

The most important thing you can do is talk with your service member about how you feel about your career, and make sure that he views your professional aspirations as equal to his own. Many service members have a tough time with this discussion because they feel like the spouse is attacking his job in the military, so reassure him that you understand you may have to relocate with his job. In return, he simply needs to be supportive of your career goals and assist you emotionally and logistically with those inevitable career transitions whenever possible. When you relocate, moving duties should be shared equally so that both of you can make your respective career transitions. Do not agree to handle moving duties instead of pursuing career goals just because Hubby wants to check in early!

During this discussion with your service member, and on your own time, begin to develop a strategy for your own career track. This strategy should cover a long period of time, not only your service member's commitment to military service but also his transition to the civilian world. In addition, it should take into account your family planning goals.

Your first strategy is to identify a career track that is portable. You want to be able to take your job skills from base to base and quickly find a job. Teaching, medical, IT, and accounting are terrific and common examples of portable careers because every military community needs them. Retail sales, hairdressing, and office management also are good choices.

Second, identify national and international companies that need your job skills and would be willing to relocate your job (and benefits) with you. Defense contractors such as Boeing, Raytheon, and General Dynamics have offices on or nearby most American military bases in the world.

WAR STORIES

Cutting-Edge Hairstyling in the Rural Florida Panhandle

My girlfriend Marie was trained as a hairstylist in the top salons of Miami Beach. When she had kids and relocated to the Florida Panhandle, she saw it as the perfect opportunity to leave the office politics of the salon and open one in her own home. Because I knew Marie as a friend, I was reluctant to ask her to cut my hair, even though all the wives were her clients. After three months of bad haircuts and juggling a newborn baby, I finally decided to call Marie and schedule an appointment. I quickly learned why she had established such a great clientele through word of mouth and was regularly booked solid.

Public relations agencies, management consulting firms, and accounting firms also have offices worldwide. In fact, my girlfriend Kendra worked for almost three years for a Boston-based public relations agency from her home near Marine Corps Base Miramar in San Diego. The agency paid to equip her home office, and they couldn't be more pleased to add a "San Diego headquarters" address to their letterhead. Kendra enjoyed her career progress and the flexibility of working from home.

The federal government is the ultimate portable employer, and military spouses receive preferential treatment for jobs. Every military base employs a small contingent of government employees to fulfill the basic needs of that community. The very services you've read about in this book, plus all kinds of jobs in quality control, secretarial pools, and management are filled by qualified applicants like yourself—many of them military wives. The trick to government employment is just getting in the door. Completing the civil service application is no small feat. However, if you find a government office that really wants to hire you, it will help you with the paperwork. And once you're in the civil service, you're in! You'll have a leg up on government jobs everywhere.

If your ambitions are larger than what is described here, I strongly encourage you to join a burgeoning new line of spouse entrepreneurs. These amazing women have opened their own lucrative businesses in a portable field of their choice and simply move the business from place to place. Is it risky? Yes, but it also can be substantially more lucrative than if you were to stay in one place. And instead of job security, you get the benefit of never having to work for another incompetent boss again!

The new generation of spouse entrepreneurs is creative beyond measure. While the military community has always had its share of profitable Avon ladies, Pampered Chefs, and Tupperware parties, the women of this new breed are running their own businesses in personal accounting, hairdressing, cleaning services, day care, freelance journalism, and marketing and public relations. Oftentimes they gained their experience from a previous employer, discovered they could run their own business better, and opened up shop from their home at half the rates their former employer was charging. With a bit of marketing, new clients come around. Better yet, with today's technology, many businesses can maintain current clients by communicating via the Internet, phone, and fax machine while moving from location to location.

WAR STORIES

Road Warrior

My girlfriend Victoria is the ultimate independent virtual assistant. In her pajamas, and in the luxury of her own home, she provides secretarial support services to several businesspeople all over the country. When she and her husband relocated to Alaska, she continued her work on the road by simply plugging in her laptop at rest stops. She says that her clients don't mind her family's frequent relocations because they don't see it and it never affects them. All they care about is the excellent assistance she provides, and they pay her well for it, too.

Education

Education is one of the best ways by which military wives adjust their careers to a portable route. Besides, many of us marry so young that we need to finish our college degree, and sometimes the most convenient time is while he is deployed. The pay and benefits sections later in this book will review the education options available to service members *and* their spouses, so don't miss out on your opportunity.

So there are a multitude of options for keeping your career alive and thriving, including many family-friendly opportunities. Again, the emphasis should be on what makes you happy by fulfilling your professional and financial aspirations. Time and again, I've heard wives complain that their hubby's military career destroyed their own career. Bullfeathers! Yes, it is more difficult to maintain a career. In the end, however, those wives allowed their own careers to fall to pieces, and their sense of self-esteem with it.

The Least You Need to Know

> You can maintain a career while relocating around the world! It just takes savvy and planning!

> Don't underestimate the importance of your career to your self-esteem, or treat it as less important than your service member's career. If your job satisfies you, don't rob yourself of happiness by putting your career track last. You'll make yourself and your family miserable.

> Most career-oriented military wives follow one of three paths: Hone their job skills to a portable career track; work for defense contractors or the government so they can simply transfer when relocating; or start their own business.

RESOURCES

> www.usajobs.gov—USAJOBS is the federal government's official one-stop source for federal jobs and employment information. Includes application forms for downloading.

> Visit your base website for local job listings.
> www.wahm.com and www.HomeBasedWorkingMoms.com—Online magazines with job boards for work-at-home moms.
> Small Business Administration—www.sba.gov
> WomenEntrepreneur.com—www.womenentrepreneur.com
> SCORE—www.score.org
> MyOwnBusiness—www.myownbusiness.org
> HireMyMom.com—www.HireMyMom.com
> EDirectory of Homebased Careers—www.eDirectoryofHomeBased Careers.com

CHAPTER 7

Personal Finances— Military Style

How Military Pay Works

Military service members get a paycheck every two weeks, just like the rest of the world. However, it's important to be aware that the amount paid can vary from paycheck to paycheck. Reservists, too, can see their pay vary substantially. To understand why and how to maximize your service member's income potential, you need to understand the components of military pay. Please note that any dollar amounts listed below are 2009 rates.

> *Basic Pay.* This is the primary source of your service member's income and is based on his pay grade (e.g., E-3 or O-1). Congress has increased Basic Pay by approximately 4 percent each year in recent years, although when the military is less politically popular, pay increases may hover around 2 percent. Historically, any increase in Basic Pay goes into effect on January 1. All Basic Pay is taxable income, and the amount of years in service or a promotion increases this pay. Marriage or your husband's service record does not affect it.

> *Basic Allowance for Housing (BAH).* BAH is what the military pays those on active duty to maintain their living quarters, including (allegedly) your utilities. You receive BAH only if you live in civilian housing; you do not receive BAH if you live in base housing. Your BAH is primar-

ily determined by the cost of living in your area, so major cities and overseas locations typically have higher BAH rates than rural areas. BAH also is adjusted by pay grade and according to whether the service member is permitted to live off base or has a family or is married—but don't necessarily expect a big jump! In some cases, the difference between BAH with dependents and BAH without dependents can be as little as $50 to $100 per month. BAH is not taxable income.

Did You Know?

BAH is the *only* regular pay that increases when a service member gets married—and not necessarily by much. Service members received Family Separation Pay only when on deployment. Contrary to popular belief, a married service member does not get any extra pay for having children, so don't go crazy with family life!

> *Basic Allowance for Subsistence (**BAS**).* This is what the military pays for feeding the service member—not for feeding the entire family. That is an important distinction because, although BAS increases somewhat when a service member does not have a meal card at the chow hall, it is nearly all docked when he deploys, since the military is now feeding him. BAS is the top reason why families get into financial trouble when the service member deploys, because they don't anticipate the $100 to $200 reduction in monthly pay. BAS is a flat rate for both officers ($223 per month) and enlisted ($324 per month) and is not taxable income.

Did You Know?

A service member loses BAS money for every day the military pays to feed him in the chow hall. If he deploys for 30 days, he loses all his BAS for that month.

> *Hardship Duty Pay.* This is a bonus of $50 to $150 per month for serving in difficult areas, either on deployment or in remote locations (e.g., an unaccompanied tour to South Korea). This income was declared nontaxable by Congress.

> *Hazardous Duty and Imminent Danger/Hostile Fire Pay.* This is exactly what you think it is. When your service member faces a dangerous situation, he gets $225 per month for it. This income is nontaxable.

> *Family Separation Allowance (FSA).* If your service member is away from home consistently for 30 days or more, you are entitled to $250 per month in FSA.

Did You Know?

If your service member is sent into the field for 28 days and then comes home for the weekend, you don't get the Family Separation Allowance. He must be gone all 30 days.

Once you understand the fundamentals of pay, you get into areas of specialty pay, all of which depend on the job skills and job situation of your service member. Bottom line: The more training he has and the more difficult the circumstances are, the more he is paid.

> *Career Sea Pay.* From $100 to $600 per month in extra pay is given to sailors and Marines attached to a ship for more than 30 days. Increases in sea pay are based on pay grade as well as accrued years of sea duty, and the income is taxable.

> *Aviation, Submarine, and Other Special Incentive Pay.* This is how the military increases compensation for learning a critical skill. Monitor these payments carefully because your service member's job choices greatly affect how much Special Pay you receive. Submarine Pay, for example, is among the highest, at an extra $75 to $835 per month. In-

creases in Special Incentive Pay are based on pay grade as well as years in service. This pay is taxable.

> *Special Duty Pay.* This is pay designated by the Secretary of Defense for duties considered to be extremely difficult or involving an unusual degree of responsibility. Although this pay is geared more toward drill instructors and recruiters, in wartime it applies to many deployed service members. Usually $100 or more per month, this pay is taxable.

> *Overseas and Continental United States (**CONUS**) Cost-of-Living Allowance (**COLA**).* You can get big bucks for living overseas or in Alaska or Hawaii, especially in less popular or high-cost places such as Japan. The Overseas COLA is also adjusted by pay grade, and it is not taxable.

Did You Know?

You get big bucks in your Cost-of-Living Allowance and Overseas Housing Allowance for living overseas! My girlfriend Kay Ann received an extra $1,000 per month while living in Iwakuni, Japan.

Other payments include:

> *Dislocation Allowance (**DLA**).* Worth up to several thousand dollars, DLA is critical in helping you cover the cost of relocating your family to a new permanent duty station. Given that the average military family loses $800 per move, it's important that you know how much DLA you'll be receiving so you can budget and plan for your trip. This is one to nag your hubby about. This income cannot be taxed.

> *Per Diem Pay for Temporary Duty (**TDY**).* If your service member goes on a business trip or is asked to do temporary duty more than 50 miles from home, he is not expected to pay the cost out of pocket. Instead, he will be given Per Diem pay, which is a daily money allowance to cover

the cost of housing and food while he is away from home. As such, this income is nontaxable. Make sure your service member arranges for Per Diem pay and saves whatever receipts necessary to have his expenses reimbursed. As an alternative, he should use the government-issued credit card. You don't want to pay for his trip on your personal credit card and have it accumulating interest while the bean counters take their sweet time figuring out how much to pay you back.

> *Reenlistment Bonus and Other Retention Bonuses.* This requires some negotiation with your Job Guy, but service members on active duty can earn up to tens of thousands of dollars just for reenlistment. Be sure to find out what your husband's colleagues have negotiated before you begin discussions with the Job Guy, or you may be missing out. There may be extra bucks for service members with critically needed skills as an incentive to stay in the service. Also, please note that your bonus is taxable, so don't spend it all.

> *Uniform Allowance.* This once-per-year nontaxable stipend for enlisted service members covers the cost of uniforms and other mandatory purchases related to your service member's job. The amount ranges between $266 and $659 per year, and those in special units such as the Army Band get extra money. Officers get this allowance only at the beginning of their career and are expected to maintain the cost of their uniforms out of their own pockets. Warning: Do not spend this money on anything but uniform items! You will end up spending every cent of this pay ensuring your service member is properly attired so he doesn't get in trouble during inspections.

Reserve Pay

Reservists just doing their usual weekend drilling typically do four drills per weekend over two days. Each drill is supposed to represent one day on active duty, because the military recognizes that Reservists tend to cram in a lot over that weekend. They are paid per drill based on their pay grade and cumulative years in service. Thus, an E-4 with more than two years of service gets $256 for four drills of playing warrior over the weekend. Reservists also get days of pay for their extended stints with the Reserves, although they may get more in FSA and other allowances, depending on how far they must travel and whether they have a family.

Did You Know?

Thousands of Reservists lost all their savings when they were called to active duty in Operation Enduring Freedom and Operation Iraqi Freedom. Why? Their military pay was substantially less than their civilian pay, and they were forced to make up the difference from their own savings. Never be lulled into complacency by peacetime. Always save at least six months' of the difference between military and civilian pay, in case your Reservist is called to active duty.

A Reservist called to active duty (or "activated") receives the same pay and allowances as a regular active duty service member. However, each command determines what the Reservist deserves, including BAH and FSA—so double-check that your service member is getting what he should.

More important, your Reservist's military pay may be substantially less than what he was receiving in his civilian job, which he now has to leave. Prepare yourself for the prospect of active duty! Calculate the difference between your civilian and military pay, and save at least six months of that amount to use in case of an emergency.

Equally important, monitor his job benefits. If your service member is activated, one of the most important things he can do is immediately sign his family up for Tricare health insurance. Additionally, know that there is a 45-day wait before Tricare kicks in that leaves families in the lurch if there is an emergency.

How to Read a Leave and Earnings Statement (Pay Stub)

Now that you understand the components of military pay, you can find out how much your service member should be earning each month by visiting CinCHouse.com's Military Pay Estimator. This powerful pay calculator has been endorsed and used by the Navy–Marine Corps Relief Society for budget counseling purposes, so you know it gives an accurate estimate of your pay. It's also a great way to project your future income if you expect significant changes in your life, such as marriage, promotion, deployment, or relocation, or to double-check to see if the DoD is paying your hardworking hubby the right amount.

Once you've calculated what the monthly pay should be, take a good look at your service member's pay stub, also known as a Leave and Earnings Statement (**LES**). You also can find his current LES and next month's predictions of pay on the **DFAS** (Defense Finance and Accounting Service) website at www.mypay.dfas.mil. Insist that your service member gets a password for this website ASAP because you'll rely on it every time you update your monthly budget and pay the bills. The total amount of your monthly income should match the Military Pay Estimator. If it does not, review each component to find the differences.

The LES will also show any **allotments**. An allotment is a certain amount of money deducted from your pay and directly paid to specified persons such as your landlord (for rent payments) or creditors. If you have bad credit, some stores will insist on being paid by allotment if you are making a large purchase.

In the old days, a deployed service member would set aside an allotment to his wife to ensure that she had enough money to pay the bills while he was gone. Although some military financial counselors still recommend doing this, there is no reason to do so as long as the wife has access to a joint checking account that receives his pay by direct deposit. Changing a checking account or direct deposit can be done almost instantly, whereas it takes a visit to command admin and several pay periods before you can end an allotment.

Sample LES for Army, Navy, and Air Force

DEFENSE FINANCE AND ACCOUNTING SERVICE MILITARY LEAVE AND EARNINGS STATEMENT

ID	NAME (LAST, FIRST, MI)	SOC. SEC. NO.	GRADE	PAY DATE	YRS SVC	ETS	BRANCH	ADSN/DSSN	PERIOD COVERED
	1	2	3	4	5	6	7	8	9

ENTITLEMENTS
TYPE	AMOUNT
	10

DEDUCTIONS
TYPE	AMOUNT
	11

ALLOTMENTS
TYPE	AMOUNT
	12

SUMMARY
+ AMT FWD	13
+ TOT ENT	14
- TOT DED	15
- TOT ALMT	16
= NET AMT	17
- CR FWD	18
= EOM PAY	19

TOTAL 20

	DIEMS	RET PLAN		
	23	24		

LEAVE

BF BAL	ERND	USED	CR BAL	ETS BAL	LV LOST	LV PAID	USE/LOSE
25	26	27	28	29	30	31	32

FED TAXES

WAGE PERIOD	WAGE YTD	M/S	EX	ADDL TAX	TAX YTD
33	34	35	36	37	38

FICA TAXES

WAGE PERIOD	SOC WAGE YTD	SOC TAX YTD	MED WAGE YTD	MED TAX YTD
39	40	41	42	43

STATE TAXES

ST	WAGE PERIOD	WAGE YTD	M/S	EX	TAX YTD
44	45	46	47	48	49

PAY DATA

BAQ TYPE	BAQ DEPN	VHA ZIP	RENT AMT	SHARE	STAT	JFTR	DEPNS	2D JFTR	BAS TYPE	CHARITY YTD	TPC	PACIDN
50	51	52	53	54	55	56	57	58	59	60	61	62

BASE PAY RATE	BASE PAY CURRENT	SPEC PAY RATE	SPEC PAY CURRENT	INC PAY RATE	INC PAY CURRENT	BONUS PAY RATE	BONUS PAY CURRENT
63	64	65	66	67	68	69	70

Thrift Savings Plan (TSP)

CURRENTLY NOT USED							
71	TSP YTD DEDUCTIONS 72	DEFERRED 73	EXEMPT 74	CURRENTLY NOT USED 75			

REMARKS

YTD ENTITLE 77	YTD DEDUCT 78
76	

DFAS Form 702, Jan 02

www.dfas.mil

Source: DFAS

─────────────── *Did You Know?* ───────────────

Military pay changes as frequently as every month, depending on your service member's circumstances. If your service member does training, deploys, relocates, does hardship duty, or has any other changes in circumstances, prevent financial trouble by re-calculating how much pay he should receive.

On pages 77 and 84 are sample Army, Navy, and Air Force Leave and Earnings Statements to show you how to interpret them. The Marine Corps version is only slightly different.

Fields 1–9 contain the identification portion of the LES.

1. NAME. The member's name in last, first, middle initial format.
2. SOC. SEC. NO. The member's Social Security number.
3. GRADE. The member's current pay grade.
4. PAY DATE. The date the member entered active duty for pay purposes in YYMMDD format. This is synonymous with the Pay Entry Base Date (PEBD).
5. YRS SVC. In two digits, the actual years of creditable service.
6. ETS. The Expiration Term of Service in YYMMDD format. This is synonymous with the Expiration of Active Obligated Service (EAOS).
7. BRANCH. The branch of service (i.e., Navy, Army, Air Force).
8. ADSN/DSSN. The Disbursing Station Symbol Number used to identify each disbursing/finance office.
9. PERIOD COVERED. This is the period covered by the individual LES. Normally it will be for one calendar month. If this is a separation LES, the separation date will appear in this field.

Fields 10–24 contain the entitlements, deductions, allotments, and their respective totals; a mathematical summary portion; date initially entered military service; and retirement plan.

10. ENTITLEMENTS. In columnar style, the names of the entitlements and allowances being paid. Space is allocated for 15 entitlements and/or allowances. If more than 15 are present, the overflow will be printed in the REMARKS block. Any retroactive entitlements and/or allowances will be added to like entitlements and/or allowances.

11. DEDUCTIONS. The descriptions of the deductions are listed in columnar style. This includes items such as taxes, SGLI, midmonth pay, and dependent dental plan. Space is allocated for 15 deductions. If more than 15 are present, the overflow will be printed in the REMARKS block. Any retroactive deductions will be added to like deductions.

12. ALLOTMENTS. In columnar style, the type of the actual allotments being deducted. This includes discretionary and nondiscretionary allotments for savings and/or checking accounts, insurance, bonds, etc. Space is allocated for 15 allotments. If a member has more than one of the same type of allotment, the only differentiation may be that of the dollar amount.

13. + AMT FWD. The amount of all unpaid pay and allowances due from the prior LES.

14. + TOT ENT. The figure from Field 20, which is the total of all entitlements and/or allowances listed.

15. – TOT DED. The figure from Field 21, which is the total of all deductions.

16. – TOT ALMT. The figure from Field 22, which is the total of all allotments.

17. = NET AMT. The dollar value of all unpaid pay and allowances, plus total entitlements and/or allowances, minus deductions and allotments due on the current LES.

18. – CR FWD. The dollar value of all unpaid pay and allowances due to reflect on the next LES as the + AMT FWD.

19. = EOM PAY. The actual amount of the payment to be paid to the member on end-of-month payday.

20–22. TOTAL. The total amounts for the entitlements and/or allowances, deductions, and allotments, respectively.

23. DIEMS. Date initially entered military service: This date is used solely to indicate which retirement plan a member is under. For

those members with a DIEMS date prior to September 8, 1980, they are under the Final Pay retirement plan. For those members with a DIEMS date of September 8, 1980, through July 31, 1986, they are under the High-3 retirement plan. For those members with a DIEMS date of August 1, 1986, or later, they were initially under the REDUX retirement plan. This was changed by law in October 2000, when they were placed under the High-3 plan, with the option to return to the REDUX plan. In consideration of making this election, they become entitled to a $30,000 Career Status Bonus. The data in this block comes from PERSCOM. DFAS is not responsible for the accuracy of this data. If a member feels that the DIEMS date shown in this block is erroneous, he must see his local servicing personnel office for corrective action.

24. RET PLAN. Type of retirement plan (i.e., Final Pay, High-3, REDUX, or Choice). (Choice reflects members who have less than 15 years of service and have not elected to go with REDUX or stay with their current retirement plan.)

Fields 25–32 contain leave (vacation time) information.

25. BF BAL. The brought-forward leave balance. Balance may be from the beginning of the fiscal year, or when active duty began, or the day after the member was paid Lump Sum Leave (LSL).
26. ERND. The cumulative amount of leave earned in the current fiscal year or current term of enlistment if the member reenlisted/extended since the beginning of the fiscal year. Normally increases by 2.5 days each month.
27. USED. The cumulative amount of leave used in the current fiscal year or current term of enlistment if member reenlisted/extended since the beginning of the fiscal year.
28. CR BAL. The current leave balance as of the end of the period covered by the LES.
29. ETS BAL. The projected leave balance to the member's Expiration Term of Service (ETS).
30. LV LOST. The number of days of leave that have been lost.
31. LV PAID. The number of days of leave paid to date.

32. USE/LOSE. The projected number of days of leave that will be lost if not taken in the current fiscal year on a monthly basis. The number of days of leave in this block will decrease with any leave usage.

Fields 33–38 contain federal tax withholding information.

33. WAGE PERIOD. The amount of money earned this LES period that is subject to Federal Income Tax Withholding (FITW).
34. WAGE YTD. The money earned year-to-date that is subject to FITW.
35. M/S. The marital status used to compute the FITW.
36. EX. The number of exemptions used to compute the FITW.
37. ADD'L TAX. The member-specified additional dollar amount to be withheld in addition to the amount computed by the marital status and exemptions.
38. TAX YTD. The cumulative total of FITW withheld throughout the calendar year.

Fields 39–43 contain Federal Insurance Contributions Act (FICA) information.

39. WAGE PERIOD. The amount of money earned this LES period that is subject to FICA.
40. SOC WAGE YTD. The wages earned year-to-date that are subject to FICA.
41. SOC TAX YTD. Cumulative total of FICA withheld throughout the calendar year.
42. MED WAGE YTD. The wages earned year-to-date that are subject to Medicare.
43. MED TAX YTD. Cumulative total of Medicare taxes paid year-to-date.

Fields 44–49 contain state tax information.

44. ST. The two-digit postal abbreviation for the state the member elected.

45. WAGE PERIOD. The amount of money earned this LES period that is subject to State Income Tax Withholding (SITW).
46. WAGE YTD. The money earned year-to-date that is subject to SITW.
47. M/S. The marital status used to compute the SITW.
48. EX. The number of exemptions used to compute the SITW.
49. TAX YTD. The cumulative total of SITW withheld throughout the calendar year.

Fields 50–62 contain additional pay data.

50. BAQ TYPE. The type of Basic Allowance for Quarters being paid.
51. BAQ DEPN. A code that indicates the type of dependent.

> A—Spouse
> C—Child
> D—Parent
> G—Grandparent
> I—Member married to member/own right
> K—Ward of the court
> L—Parents-in-law
> R—Own right
> S—Student (ages 21–22)
> T—Handicapped child over age 21
> W—Member married to member, child under age 21

52. VHA ZIP. The zip code used in the computation of Variable Housing Allowance (VHA), if entitlement exists.
53. RENT AMT. The amount of rent paid for housing, if applicable.
54. SHARE. The number of people with whom the member shares housing costs.
55. STAT. The VHA status (i.e., accompanied or unaccompanied).
56. JFTR. The Joint Federal Travel Regulation (JFTR) code, based on the location of the member for Cost of Living Allowance (COLA) purposes.

57. DEPNS. The number of dependents the member has for VHA purposes.

58. 2D JFTR. The JFTR code based on the location of the member's dependents for COLA purposes.

59. BAS TYPE. An alpha code that indicates the type of Basic Allowance for Subsistence (BAS) the member is receiving, if applicable. This field will be blank for officers.

> B—Separate Rations
> C—TDY/PCS/Proceed Time
> H—Rations-in-kind not available
> K—Rations under emergency conditions

60. CHARITY YTD. The cumulative amount of charitable contributions for the calendar year.

61. TPC. This field is not used by the active component of any branch of service.

62. PACIDN. The activity Unit Identification Code (UIC). This field is currently used by the Army only.

Fields 63–75 contain Thrift Savings Plan (TSP) information/data.

63. BASE PAY RATE. The percentage of base pay elected for TSP contributions.

64. BASE PAY CURRENT. Reserved for future use.

65. SPECIAL PAY RATE. The percentage of Special Pay elected for TSP contributions.

66. SPECIAL PAY CURRENT. Reserved for future use.

67. INCENTIVE PAY RATE. Percentage of Incentive Pay elected for TSP contributions.

68. INCENTIVE PAY CURRENT. Reserved for future use.

69. BONUS PAY RATE. The percentage of Bonus Pay elected toward TSP contributions.

70. BONUS PAY CURRENT. Reserved for future use.

71. Reserved for future use.

Sample LES for Marine Corps

MARINE CORPS TOTAL FORCE LEAVE AND EARNINGS STATEMENT

A ID DIST RUC INFO	1 NAME (LAST, FIRST, MI)	2 SSN	3 RANK	4 SERV	5 PLT CODE	6 DATE PREP	7 PRD COVERED	8 FEBD	9 YRS	0 EAS	11 ECC	12 MCC

B FORCAST AMOUNTS	13 DATE	AMOUNT 14 DATE	AMOUNT	C SPLIT PAY	15 START DATE	16 AMOUNT	17 BALANCE	18 POE	D DIRECT DEPOSIT/EFT/ADDRESS

E LEAVE INFORMATION

19 LV BF INFORMATION	20 EARNED USED	21	22 EXCESS	23 BAL	24 MAX ACCRUAL	25 LOST	26 SOLD/AS OF	27 CBT LV BAL	28 OFFICER BASE DATE

F AVIATION PAY INFORMATION

29 AVIATOR BASE DATE	30 FLY TIME	31 ACCUM OP FLY TIME YRS MO	32 OP FLY GATE BASE DATE

G TAX INFORMATION

GOVERNMENT

H RIGHTS OF MARINES INDEBTED TO THE GOVERNMENT

YOU HAVE THE RIGHT TO:
- Inspect and copy records pertaining to debt
- Question validity of a debt and submit refuting evidence
- Negotiate a repayment schedule
- Request a waiver of debt

More information about your rights can be obtained from your Commanding Officer via your Chain of Command.

33 STATE TAX	34 FEDERAL TAX
STATE CODE EXEMPTIONS	EXEMPTIONS
WAGES THIS PRD	WAGES THIS PRD
WAGES YTD	WAGES YTD
STATE TAX YTD	FED TAX YTD

35 FICA (SOCIAL SECURITY TAX)
SSEC WAGES THIS PRD
SSEC WAGES YTD
SSEC TAX YTD
MEDICARE WAGES THIS PRD
MEDICARE WAGES YTD
MEDICARE TAX YTD

I ADDITIONAL BAH INFORMATION

INFO	37 BAH ZIP	38	39	40	41	42
36						

J CAREER SEA PAY

43 DATE	TOTAL CAREER SEA SVC

K EDUCATION DEDUCTION

44 TYPE	45 MONTHLY AMT	46 TOTAL
YRS MO DA		

L ADMIN

47 PAY STATUS

M RESERVE DRILL INFORMATION

	48 PAY	49 CRA DATE GROUP
REG	52 REG	53	54 ADD	55 ADD	56 ADD	57 BF
DSSN	PFTD	ANNYTD	PFTD	ANNYTD	ANNYTD	

N RESERVE RETIREMENT INFORMATION

REG	58 ACDU THIS PRD	59 DRILL THIS PRD	60 OTHER THIS PRD	61 MBR THIS PRD	62 END BAL THIS PRD	63 TOTAL SAT YRS	64 TOTAL RET PTS	65 RESERVE ECC
							50	

O REMARKS

DFAS-KC 7220/39 (REV 2-9_)   WWW.DFAS.MIL   ETT INFO:DFAS-KC 1-800-449-3327

DFAS-KC-KC 1-888-449-3327

Source: DFAS

72. TSP YTD DEDUCTION. Dollar amount of TSP contributions deducted for the year to date.

73. DEFERRED. Total dollar amount of TSP contributions that are deferred for tax purposes.

74. EXEMPT. Dollar amount of TSP contributions that are reported as tax exempt to the Internal Revenue Service.

75. Reserved for future use.

76. REMARKS. This area is used to provide you with general notices from varying levels of command, as well as the literal explanation of starts, stops, and changes to pay items in the entries within the ENTITLEMENTS, DEDUCTIONS, and ALLOTMENTS fields.

77. YTD ENTITLE. The cumulative total of all entitlements for the calendar year.

78. YTD DEDUCT. The cumulative total of all deductions for the calendar year.

The Marine Corps LES has a slightly different format than the other services, but the same acronyms and categories apply.

Taxable vs. Nontaxable Income

It may seem like nitpicking because the information will appear automatically on the service member's annual W-2 tax form, but it's important to know how much of your income is taxable vs. nontaxable because it affects your tax withholding and helps you compare a military salary against a civilian salary. To determine an equivalent civilian salary, multiply your nontaxable income by approximately 30 percent—or the amount the government would tax you—and add that to your total salary. For example, if your service member earns $15,000 per year in taxable income and $15,000 per year in nontaxable income, he is actually earning the civilian equivalent of $34,500—not $30,000. You can also get tax benefits from certain states.

Problems with Military Pay

Like all human beings, the military bureaucracy sometimes makes mistakes in pay, especially when the service member has recently entered the military, relocated, or been promoted. It is in your best interest to watch out for overpayments as well as underpayments. Whatever you do, do not spend an overpayment, because someday the government will find out, and it will dock your pay the full amount until the money is paid back. Many a family has walked into financial counseling because they weren't aware of an overpayment—or multiple overpayments—and were docked pay for months at a time because they couldn't pay it back.

Pay miscalculations happen in all components of military pay, but especially in those areas that change during relocation and deployment. If you think you have a pay problem, start by determining how much you should be paid on the CinCHouse.com Military Pay Estimator. Cross-check that amount on your service member's LES. If you find a discrepancy, have your hubby verify and correct it immediately with his command admin, who will work with your personnel office or the Disbursement Office, both of which work with DFAS's central office. Finally, if you find yourself in a pickle because of an accounting error, visit a financial services organization such as the Navy–Marine Corps Relief Society. It can provide you with an interest-free loan to help you survive paying back money or cover you in case of underpayment.

Direct Deposit

In this day and age, everyone should be receiving his or her pay via direct deposit into a checking account, but this is particularly important for military families. Some special payments and bonuses, particularly those related to relocation, temporary duty, and deployment, are not paid in advance with your biweekly paycheck. Instead, they are often paid at the last minute. With direct deposit, you are ensuring the money goes directly into your checking account when you need it instead of worrying about when—or whether—a check will arrive in the mail before you begin traveling.

Tax and Regulatory Benefits

Many states treat military service members quite favorably when it comes to other taxes and regulations. Automobiles and state residency are the biggest examples. Armed with this knowledge, you can take advantage of the benefits.

Your service member's state residency should be a matter of financial savvy, not emotional attachment to his hometown. Military service members are exempt from having to reestablish their legal residency every time they move, so they can choose their legal state of residence, even if they haven't lived there in 20 years or if they initially lived there for only a few months. The key to establishing legal residency is getting a driver's license and registering to vote in that particular state. Many service members deliberately establish their residence in states such as Florida, Texas, and Pennsylvania to avoid paying high income taxes elsewhere, particularly in states such as California.

Military spouses are not so lucky. We are forced to change our state residency every time we relocate and pay taxes in that state. This causes more problems than just having to calculate taxes for two states in a year in which you have relocated. If a car is registered or coregistered in your name, you are required to reregister it in your new state and pay taxes on it. For this reason, many military couples opt to keep their cars in the service member's name only. Again, the service member will carefully select a state of residence that has low automobile taxes.

Going back to the issue of financial benefits for hazardous duty, service members receive significant tax relief if the Internal Revenue Service

---

Did You Know?

Most couples opt to register property such as cars in the name of a service member only to prevent having to reregister the vehicles and pay higher taxes with every move. If you think you may be headed for divorce, however, change the registration to list yourself as co-owner. While most divorce courts will recognize the spouse as co-owner, it's better to be safe than sorry.

(**IRS**) deems them as performing "qualified hazardous duty" in a designated Combat Zone. This exemption is called the "Combat Tax Exclusion" and is determined by Congress or the president. Typically, this status is designated for wartime or dangerous peacekeeping operations, and it means that all enlisted and warrant officer pay earned while in that duty station is not subject to federal and state income tax. Officers' pay not subject to tax is capped at the highest amount of enlisted pay plus Imminent Danger Pay, and the rest is taxable. So if your hubby spent six months in designated dangerous locations such as Afghanistan or the Persian Gulf, or if he is wounded in those combat areas and spends time at a medical facility, none or little of his pay for that time can be taxed by the IRS. Check the IRS website at www.irs.gov or with command admin to make sure he is qualified.

Lower Your Interest Rates by Going to War

For Reservists and recruits, the Service Members' Civil Relief Act (**SSCRA**) can also bring you a reduction in your mortgage interest rates and other loans—a critical savings for Reservists in particular, since they are most likely to see their income plummet when they leave their civilian jobs and go on active duty for an extended period. Recruits, too, can also get interest rates on debt acquired before entering the military reduced to 6 percent. When the SSCRA is invoked during wartime or near-wartime situations, the Department of Housing and Urban Development (**HUD**) sends a letter to all FHA-approved mortgage lenders advising them of their obligations under this act, namely that they must reduce their mortgage interest rates to no more than 6 percent for loans to military on active duty (including Guard and Reserve). The SSCRA also:

> Prohibits lenders from foreclosing on service members during and immediately following their tour of active duty.
> Reduces rates on preexisting credit card debt.
> Prevents eviction if your rent is less than $1,200 per month.
> Can delay all civil court proceedings, including bankruptcy and divorce.

The military recommends that you send notice in writing to all lenders if you plan to invoke the 6 percent cap on interest rates, and keep a copy for yourself. For more information, call HUD at 1-888-297-8685 or go to the HUD website at www.hud.gov. Better yet, send your service member to the Judge Advocate General's (JAG's) office to get a sample letter. The JAG will also help you combat lenders who are refusing to obey the law.

Retirement Benefits

Service members on active duty or in the Reserves or National Guard may retire with pensionlike benefits after a minimum of 20 years of service. Disabled service members also may be medically retired prior to 20 years. Simply leaving active duty after five years of service does not make you a "retiree." Retirees receive monthly income from the government for life and may continue to receive important benefits, such as medical care and access to services on base.

There are effectively two retirement systems available for nondisability retirees. First is the **High-3** Year Average system, which entitles a service member to receive a percentage of his Basic Pay at his last pay grade as calculated by 2.5 percent times the number of years in service. For example, if your service member serves 30 years, he would receive 2.5% × 30, or 75 percent, of his average Basic Pay received during the 36 months when it was highest. Cost-of-living adjustments (**COLA**) are increased annually to account for increases in inflation.

The **REDUX** retirement system is more controversial because it offers a $30,000 Career Status Bonus to service members in their 15th year of employment if they commit to 20 years of service. Those who don't complete that commitment must pay back a prorated share of the bonus. The bonus is considered to be taxable income unless placed in a tax-free investment, such as an Individual Retirement Account (IRA). The retirement multiplier is reduced to 2 percent for those serving 20 years, although it goes back up to 3.5 percent for those serving as long as 30 years. However, at age 62, the retirement multiplier is recalculated to come on par with the High-3 multiplier. And the COLA is less than what is offered in High-3, effectively the inflation rate (Consumer Price Index or CPI) minus 1 percent.

In the end, those who accept REDUX over the High-3 retirement system must decide early—at the 15-year mark in their career—that they plan to stay for the full 30 years to maximize their benefits. Further, they take on the added risk that the COLA may not keep up with the pace of inflation, so their personal retirement savings would have to cover the gap through the duration of their retirement. The key is to ask yourself whether you would invest the $30,000 bonus or spend it. Investing it ensures your long-term retirement income and possibly an inheritance for your child; spending the money could spell disaster and poverty for REDUX retirees. So be honest with yourself and talk to a financial planner before making this important choice.

The Thrift Savings Plan (**TSP**) is an additional and voluntary retirement savings plan originally created for federal civilian employees and extended to military service members in 2000. It is ultimately intended to replace the old retirement system by acting like a 401(k) plan. Every year, your service member puts away a certain amount of money, a portion of Basic Pay and 100 percent of Special and Bonus Pay not to exceed $16,500 annually (in 2009 numbers), in a specified mutual fund monitored by the TSP administrators. There are six investment funds to choose from, ranging from conservative to aggressive in their approach and rate of return. The money invested is not taxed as income that year, which reduces your tax burden, and over time your retirement savings grow in the private stock and bond markets. The income you receive in retirement depends upon how much you have invested and your rate of return, and you will receive those benefits no matter when you retire or leave the military.

TSP is not a perfect retirement plan in that it doesn't allow spouses to participate and the government does not match most service members' contributions dollar for dollar, the way many civilian employers do. But it's a terrific way to ensure that you and your hubby have enough money to retire someday, even if Congress doesn't fully fund the retirement benefits you were promised. For more information, visit www.tsp.gov.

———————— *Did You Know?* ————————

The government issues traveling service members a credit card and asks that they charge all travel-related expenses on it. Watch out! Do not put personal charges on the credit card, and be sure to pay off all charges with your reimbursement. The card goes on your personal credit report, and you could get in trouble financially and with the military.

How Politics Affects Your Retirement

Did you notice that, in the creation and emphasis of the REDUX system over the High-3 system, the Department of Defense is trying to "preload" your retirement savings so that the stock market—and not taxpayer money—is funding your retirement? That's because, within the next 30 years, the federal government will no longer be able to afford to pay for all of the retirement promises it has made to employees and Social Security recipients. Instead, they are hoping everyone will create their own retirement savings to fund each individual retirement, rather than rely on a DoD pension or Social Security benefit.

It sounds insane to offer such massive retirement benefits that you cannot afford to pay out—but that's Congress for you. And Congress is now scrambling to fix the problem. Unfortunately, Congress is also responsible for the yearly cost-of-living adjustments (COLAs) that are supposed to increase your retirement income to keep up with inflation. The reality, however, is that COLAs decrease when the military is not politically popular and increase when it is. As the population of veterans decreases with the passing of the World War II generation, be aware that your retirement benefits may wane with the political will of Congress. In the end, you need to save for your own retirement.

Survivor's Benefits and Life Insurance

While the military does not provide a retirement savings option for military spouses, it does provide some survivor's benefits to spouses of military personnel who die on active duty or when death is due to a service-related disability.

According to the Department of Veterans' Affairs, the Survivor's Benefit Plan (**SBP**) payments are equal to 55 percent of what a member's retirement pay would have been had he or she been retired at 100 percent disability. A surviving spouse will also receive a flat amount of $1,081 per month of Dependency and Indemnity Compensation (**DIC**). However, SBP is reduced by DIC. Moreover, if the spouse remarries before age 55, SBP payments cease. There may be additional money for surviving children, but not much. If the service member had a rank of E-4 when he was killed, the family will not receive much money. Nor is an E-4 salary sufficient to cover family expenses as children grow older. Normally those expenses are covered because a service member's salary increases during the progress of his career. What this means is that **you need to have life insurance and save for your own retirement—no one else will do it for you.**

Certainly, it is difficult for spouses to save for retirement. Because we move from job to job, we're not likely to contribute to employer-sponsored retirement investments such as a 401(k) plan for any length of time. CinCHouse strongly encourages you to set up your own IRA and invest in it at least the same amount of money your husband invests in his retirement savings plan or TSP.

------------------------------ *Did You Know?* ------------------------------

The government's retirement systems, including Social Security and the military retirement system, are going broke! Better to save money for your own retirement than hope for the politicians to straighten things out.

Once you enter military life, you will be bombarded with offers for inexpensive life insurance for you and your service member. It's enough to make you wonder why.

While choosing life insurance is a complicated and personal decision, partly because it can be treated as an investment opportunity, you should know that the military provides a Death Gratuity of $100,000 within 72 hours of a service member being killed while on active duty. It also provides very inexpensive life insurance for your entire family through the duration of service. The program, entitled Service Members' Group Life Insurance (**SGLI**), provides $400,000 in coverage to active-duty service members for just $26 per month. For spouses, SGLI provides $100,000 coverage for $5.50 or less per month for ages 34 and below, and a maximum $7 per month for ages 35–44, and so on, past this age bracket. Dependent children automatically receive $10,000 coverage free of charge. While you should consider purchasing life insurance that extends beyond the duration of your service member's service (at which age life insurance becomes expensive), you'd be hard pressed to beat these rates for your immediate needs.

Educational Benefits

When most people think of educational opportunities related to the military, they think of the Montgomery G.I. Bill. This is the recruiting incentive that offers most active-duty service members and Reservists up to $28,800 in tuition in return for a three-year commitment on active duty. During that commitment, you pay $100 a month for a year, but you will get up to $985 a month for three years, which can be put to use not only for college degree programs but also for certificate programs, flight training, apprenticeship/on-the-job training, and correspondence courses.

Even better, the new post-9/11 G.I. Bill offers education benefits worth an average of $80,000—double the value of those in the previous program—for service members who served three years in the military (and a percentage for those who served less time, down to as few as 90 days). It pays approved universities or vocational schools (with associate degrees) directly for the full costs of tuition, up to the cost of the most expensive in-state tuition. It also provides a $1,000 annual stipend for books and BAH equivalent to an E-5 in that zip code. It's also transferable to family members of career service members. Service members and families are entitled to benefits of the new bill for up to 36 months and have up to 15 years from their last 30 days of continuous service to use their entitlements (see specific eligibility requirements in chapter 3).

Enrollment into the post-9/11 G.I. Bill is free. Eligibility for the Montgomery G.I. Bill is based on service commitment and requires active-duty service members to pay a $1,200 fee over the initial year of their enlistment. However, the Montgomery G.I. Bill gives benefits for nontraditional apprenticeship programs and on-the-job training. The Student Loan Repayment Program is the reverse of the Montgomery G.I. Bill, effectively paying off your student loan in return for a service commitment. For all these programs, be sure to check the latest eligibility requirements and stipulations before assuming you'll get a free education. In addition to these great opportunities, however, the military boasts a network of more than 1,800 schools for service members and spouses; it's called the Service Member Opportunity Network (**SOC**) (www.soc .aascu.org). The SOC network is especially good at allowing military couples to transfer credits between network schools, but be aware that this is most easily accomplished when you visit a college counselor in person. Of course, you should also consider the hundreds of colleges and universities that maintain representatives and/or courses on each base, the opportunities for distance learning, and the hundreds of scholarships available to service members and their spouses and children.

In the end, there is almost no excuse for any military wife or woman not to complete or continue her education. To get a list of local colleges and universities, especially those with representatives on your local military base, visit CinCHouse.com's sections on local military bases or call the career counselor at your local Family Support Center. Also, visit CinCHouse.com periodically for an update of the latest scholarship opportunities available for you or your children.

The Least You Need to Know

> Understand the components of military pay and find out how your service member's pay will vary depending on your circumstances. Don't be caught off guard by a $200 pay short.

> Check your Leave and Earnings Statement and compare it to the

CinCHouse Military Pay Estimator to see if you have any overpayments or pay shorts. Report any pay problems immediately to your command admin, and be sure not to spend any overpayments.

> Military service members receive substantial tax and regulatory benefits and creditor protections, but you have to learn about them to maximize your money.

> If your service member plans to make a career of the military, he should choose his retirement plan carefully to make sure it fits your spending habits and retirement needs.

> The Social Security and military pension systems may be going bankrupt, so it's important that you and your service member save money for retirement through the Thrift Savings Program and Individual Retirement Accounts.

> Survivor benefits for widows are a pittance, so make sure you purchase life insurance and save money of your own.

RESOURCES

> www.cinchouse.com—Find the Military Pay Estimator to calculate how much income your service member should be receiving each month depending on his circumstances.

> www.dfas.mil—Bookmark this link to the Defense Finance and Accounting Service! You'll use this site to check your service member's monthly Leave and Earnings Statements, predict next month's pay, and fix any pay problems.

> www.hud.gov—The Department of Housing and Urban Development has more information on how you can receive financial protection and lower your interest rates under the Soldiers' and Sailors' Civil Relief Act.

> www.irs.gov—The Internal Revenue Service website provides specific information for military families on how to reduce your tax burden. Make it a point to visit this site before you do your taxes every year.

> www.tsp.gov—More information on the Thrift Savings Program, which your service member should be using to save money for retirement.

> www.staynavy.navy.mil—A career development website for sailors.
> sso.mol.usmc.mil/SSO—A career development site for Marines.
> www.marinenet.usmc.mil/marinenet/—A Marine Corps portal for classes and career advancement.
> www.us.army.mil/suite/login/welcome.html—Army Knowledge Online is a career development and information site for the Army.
> www.my.af.mil—An Air Force online portal for classes and career advancement.
> Service Member Opportunity Colleges—www.soc.aascu.org.

CHAPTER 8

Health Care Benefits

For service members on active duty, the military promises them and their families virtually free health care and generally delivers. Nowhere else in the world can you deliver a baby with complete pre- and postnatal care at absolutely no cost. This care is delivered through Tricare, the military's own HMO. While some might think Tricare has a bottomless pit of funding from Congress, the program administration is actually assisted by regional private HMOs that contract with the government. As with all HMOs, getting the best medical care means understanding the system.

Myths About Military vs. Civilian Care

The first thing you'll discover about military health care is that there are military doctors and hospitals. While Tricare will allow you to see a civilian provider if you live more than 50 miles from a military base, it will typically assign you to a physician at a military treatment facility (clinic or hospital) if you have signed up for Tricare Prime.

Oh, great! you think. The same bozos who keep me waiting in line to sign papers are now providing my health care!

Actually, military doctors and nurses are exactly the same as their civilian counterparts, except they know more about military-specific issues, deploy with the troops, and relocate as frequently as you do. Doctors train in the same medical schools as civilian providers, and their specialty training certifications come from the same nationally accredited organizations as civilians. But instead of owing hundreds of thousands in student loans—paid for by patients like you—they are debt- free in exchange for serving time in the military.

In addition to going through regular medical training, military doctors and health care providers receive extra schooling in subjects such as tropical diseases and biological/chemical threats. Extra training has benefits for you, from understanding how to treat the rash your child got while in Guam to providing the first response to biological warfare with antidotes they keep on hand in their hospitals.

Finally, military doctors understand what you're going through in terms of relocation, deployment, and other issues because they go through it, too. My own case is a good example of the special treatment

WAR STORIES

Where to Go on September 11

September 11 was a terrifying day for all Americans, and many spent the following weeks trying to find gas masks and to determine which drugs they needed to stock their medicine cabinet. Talk radio hosts pondered for hours where citizens could go to protect themselves.

Most military wives had no such doubts. Not only was base security searching anything that moved, but also our hospitals and clinics were already stocked with antidotes to biological threats such as anthrax and teeming with the best-trained medical experts in the world. Besides, I defy any terrorist to go directly after a U.S. military base, especially one housing the Marines. The relish with which the Marines would respond brings a smile to my face just thinking about it.

we get in unusual circumstances. My husband and I had trouble conceiving our first child. After trying for the requisite one year, we had only three months left before we were scheduled to relocate to a training program across the country. Recognizing the trouble we would have had starting up with a new gynecologist at this stage, my gynecologist (an expert in infertility) expedited the tests and procedures needed to get me knocked up before we relocated. Two weeks before the movers came, I found out I was pregnant, and we now have a beautiful baby boy!

─────────── *Did You Know?* ───────────

If you are a new spouse and want to continue seeing your civilian physician, and you are thinking about going with Tricare Standard, you'll need to ask your physician if he accepts Tricare. Because Tricare reimburses at a rate lower than Medicare, many civilian physicians won't accept it.

While there is a priority system whereby service members are treated first, followed by families and then veterans, enlisted family members benefit the most because the system is designed to serve young families. Your primary care physician will probably be a family physician, sometimes called a "super GP" because they handle everything from delivering babies to well-baby checkups, but have significantly more training than the old-fashioned general practitioners. With family physicians, you can make one appointment for the whole family and see the same doctor every time (unless you or the doctor relocates).

In addition to primary care physicians, the military has all types of medical specialists from dermatologists to plastic surgeons; all board-certified experts in their respective fields. While the smaller military hospitals and clinics generally won't have all specialties available, Tricare and your primary care physician will ensure that you get the specialty care you need.

Alternative medicine and nontraditional providers, including chiropractors and nurse midwives, are respected and can be found at military hospitals. Some health care providers are even trained by the military in acupuncture and other holistic medicine.

Finally, the military's use of training hospitals to provide care for military families means that military doctors are on the cutting edge of medicine. As a patient, you'll receive care based on the latest scientific knowledge and the best equipment.

Tricare: The HMO for the Military

The reason why you need to understand that there are virtually no differences—and some benefits—to having a military health care provider is that such care costs substantially less than insisting on a civilian provider.

Tricare has two main types of health plans for active-duty family members: Tricare Prime and Tricare Standard. Active-duty service members themselves are covered under Prime, as are most military families. Reservists are covered by Tricare only if they are activated, and then they and their families receive the same coverage as for active duty—but be sure to jump on the paperwork to start coverage right away. Reservists are not automatically enrolled in Tricare when they are activated, so it's important for service members to sign up as soon as possible. Typically there is a 45-day gap before coverage starts.

Tricare Prime works much like a typical HMO. There are no enrollment fees, deductibles, or cost sharing (except overseas), but you are required to go through the military health system first and, if care is not available, only then can you see a civilian provider. That means that you must attempt to receive care through a Primary Care Manager (**PCM**) at a Military Treatment Facility (**MTF**) such as a Uniformed Services Hospital or clinic. If they cannot provide you with care, you are automatically referred for treatment at an approved civilian facility. If it's not approved by Tricare, you will be fully responsible for all costs associated with civilian care. You can find a civilian provider authorized by Tricare in your area by looking on the Tricare website at www.tricare.mil/; reviewing its provider booklet; calling your local Tricare representative; or, if overseas, asking the local U.S. embassy or consulate. Under Prime, you can receive

Tricare Cost Comparison Table

	Tricare Prime	Tricare Standard
Annual Deductible	None	$150 per individual or $300 per family for E-5 and above; $50/$100 for E-4 and below
Annual Enrollment Fee	None	None
Civilian Outpatient Visit	No cost	20% after annual deductible is met
Civilian Inpatient	No cost	$15.15 per day

Source: Tricare: Summary of Beneficiary Costs.

emergency care in any military or civilian facility, but you should check with and notify your MTF and/or Tricare representative. Similarly, specialty care—provided by both military and civilians—is available, but it must be managed and coordinated through your PCM. Now you understand the importance of building a good relationship with your PCM—he or she can often save you valuable time and effort in getting the care you need! Tricare Prime coverage is portable as you move from region to region (see regions and contact information on pages 109–111).

In contrast to Tricare Prime, Tricare Standard is less popular among military families because of the deductibles and cost sharing as well as more restricted access to care at a military facility. Also, unlike Prime, you or your health care provider must file your claims to subsequently be reimbursed, which means you may be carrying health care expenses on your credit card for a while. Tricare Standard is generally used by wives who want to continue using a specific civilian provider and who have other health insurance provided by their employer. Whenever Tricare beneficiaries carry a second form of insurance, Tricare becomes the secondary payer (once the annual deductible is paid) and typically covers whatever out-of-pocket expenses are not covered by the employer's insurance as long as the service is authorized by Tricare. Without the second form of insurance, however, Tricare pays only 80 percent of the authorized cost, and you pay the remaining 20 percent plus any fees that are higher than what Tricare authorizes (up to the legal limit of 15 percent above Tricare rates). Tricare Standard does have a cap on what you pay out-of-pocket for catastrophic care, as long as the services are authorized, but you must keep close track of your expenses.

Special plans for special situations are also available under Tricare, such as Tricare Prime Remote. This is the equivalent of Tricare Prime for beneficiaries who live 50 miles or one hour away from the closest MTF.

Pharmacy benefits are also included in both Tricare plans. Your out-of-pocket costs for prescription drugs are zero if you obtain your prescription at an MTF pharmacy, and you can receive 90 days' worth of the prescription. The second option is the Tricare Mail Order Pharmacy, but you can get only a 90-day supply of your prescription at a time. Contact your health care provider, or call 1-866-363-8667 in the United States or 1-866-275-4732 overseas to find out more. A third option is to use a Tricare network pharmacy, which includes most major drugstore chains. You will pay $9 for a 30-day supply of a brand-name medication, or $3 for a 30-day supply of the generic version. Finally, you can use a non-network pharmacy, but you will be reimbursed for only a portion of the cost after your annual deductible is paid. Again, it pays to use a military health facility.

How Tricare's Coverage Rates

Having spent 10 years in and out of different HMOs paid for by my civilian employers, I can attest that Tricare appears to have the same caliber of health care coverage—and often better. Government health benefits usually are. Those who complain about Tricare typically have unusual circumstances or don't understand and aren't willing to deal with the HMO system. HMOs are here to stay, folks, and Tricare is one of the better ones.

The key to obtaining coverage of your specific health care needs is the term "medically necessary." Tricare has a list of what ailments are or are not covered, but if a doctor says you need coverage, Tricare generally will give it. Military doctors and civilians who do a lot of work with Tricare understand this, and they will work with you to make sure your expenses are covered. Yet another reason to establish a good relationship with your PCM!

To my knowledge, Tricare Prime is the only HMO plan in the world where it costs nothing to have a baby, from your prenatal vitamins to your postpartum checkup. Well-baby, well-child, and well-woman visits also are covered, as are visits for mental health care, obesity, infertility, birth control, and genetic testing. There are some exceptions to coverage, such as artificial insemination and abortion (unless the mother's health is at risk), but much of it is left to the discretion of your doctor.

Maternity care is particularly generous and generally hassle-free under Tricare. If you want to go to a civilian physician for your OB care and there is an MTF available, you'll have to change to Tricare Standard and pay a copay. If you wish to use alternative methods, such as a birthing facility instead of a hospital, you have the option to do so, but with costs being shared. The only outstanding item not covered is "lay" midwives (as opposed to the medically trained and licensed superhero nurse midwives), but no insurance covers such minimally trained, nonlicensed caregivers. Doulas are welcome to attend births at MTFs.

On a final note, be sure to verify your Tricare coverage and DEERS report every year or every time you move. These guys process up to 25 million claims each year and are known for occasionally "dropping" beneficiaries out of the system. This comes as a shock when the purported beneficiary is either denied care or receives a whopping bill for health services. A once-per-year verification is worth the trouble of a phone call compared to a bureaucratic nightmare of a dropped beneficiary.

Tricks for Getting the Best Health Care

As with all HMOs, there are tricks to avoiding bureaucrats and getting the best health care available. Fortunately, as discussed earlier, the system is designed to try to connect you with one primary care provider instead of allowing you to slip through the cracks by using multiple doctors. By trying to stick with one doctor, you can build a relationship of trust so you can deal directly with him or her when issues come up instead of always having to make an appointment. Should you have an emergency, be sure to keep your family doctor informed. And should your doctor relocate, ask him or her to refer you to another doctor. You are more likely to get someone who operates along the same lines as your old doctor.

— Did You Know? —

Once you give birth or adopt, your baby is automatically covered by Tricare for the first 60 days of life. At that point, your service member must enroll the child in DEERS, which amends Page 2 of his service record to explain his expanding family, and complete a Tricare Prime enrollment form. If the child is not enrolled into Tricare Prime (or Tricare Prime Remote) by day 60, their coverage becomes Tricare Standard or Extra on day 61—which costs more in out-of-pocket expenses. Enrolling the child into Tricare Prime before day 60 will ensure continuous coverage. Don't forget to do this, or you'll be kicking yourself when your child is suddenly not eligible to see his or her doctor and you have to go through a bureaucratic hassle to rectify this.

Getting personal referrals from friends and neighbors for your family health care provider can help you identify one provider, among hundreds at any military hospital, who will understand your needs. Once you've identified a provider, call Tricare to designate him or her as your Primary Care Manager and make an appointment.

What should you do if you don't like your doctor? Switch! Ask your friends and neighbors whom they use and call Tricare to switch your PCM. The doctor will not be offended; sometimes people just don't click. What's more important is that you are comfortable with your health care provider.

What should you do if Tricare denies your request? This may sound silly, but start by simply hanging up with the bureaucrat you were speaking to, then calling back until you find a sympathetic one. Or go down to the MTF and visit the local Tricare rep. Sometimes the first bureaucrat is someone who is too young or too inexperienced to give you a good answer, whether it's the answer you want or an alternative solution to the problem. If working with other Tricare bureaucrats does not solve your problem, call your doctor and ask him to deal with Tricare. He has more clout and often can get the right answers by knowing whom to go to, what logic to use, and which buttons to push.

WAR STORIES

Birth by Long Distance?

When I was five months pregnant, I moved with my husband to a nine-week training program. Recognizing I would need two visits with the obstetrician during that time, I called up Tricare to relocate my coverage to the new region. Unfortunately, I got a young, burgeoning bureaucrat on the line who had obviously never had a baby. She typed in my zip code and—voilà!—pulled up an Air Force hospital located two hours away. When I protested at the ridiculousness of having to travel two hours, particularly if there was an emergency, she insisted that was what the rules said. So I thanked her, went to my appointment, and promptly visited the Tricare office at the hospital to vent my frustration. Sure enough, they agreed with me and gave me permission to see a civilian doctor 15 minutes from my home.

To get future appointments faster than by calling a hospital's appointment line, ask your doctor at your first meeting if there's an easier way to contact him or her for questions or appointments. Oftentimes, doctors have a nurse or other health care provider who can answer calls quickly and arrange appointments to avoid bureaucratic hassles and to provide more personal service.

If you actually call this nurse and she gives you advice instead of allowing you to talk to the doctor, don't assume that she is malevolently preventing you from doing so. Instead, she is probably discussing it briefly with the doctor behind the scenes, or perhaps she commonly deals with the situation you are presenting. By running interference for the doctor, she is helping you get advice quickly. Your only other option may be to go through the hassle of making an appointment.

Dealing with a receptionist is a different ball game than talking to a nurse. Receptionists on the hospital appointment line do not have the training to assess your medical condition, so don't expect them to. They have no medical schooling and are trained solely to guess whether you need a 15- or a 45-minute appointment with the doctor or other health care provider. Thus you need to communicate exactly that by explaining the depth of your concern. Having said that, don't waste your doctor's time by insisting on a 45-minute visit to address sinus congestion, or go to a 15-minute appointment with a huge list of ailments, or wait until the last minute to raise the real issue concerning you.

Don't be modest with your health care provider, either. Your doctor and health care providers have seen literally thousands of crotches and other private places. Anything you show them or tell them they will have seen or heard before. What is more important than your girlish modesty is getting solid health advice. So don't think you're being cute by acting squeamish or making the doctor guess what's wrong.

If you're not sure whether you should see a health care provider, call the Nurse HelpLine at either your local MTF or through Tricare. A final tip is to talk with friends and neighbors about the best care facility in your area. Major military hospitals have some of the world's leading specialists, but you may get lost in the system and have to wait for hours for your appointment. Community hospitals or satellite family clinics are often a good choice for routine care.

When a Family Member Has Special Needs

When our son was diagnosed as being on the autistic spectrum, I was pleasantly surprised to learn that we are not alone—far from it. Many military families have members with a variety of special needs, and the military has really gotten good about addressing those needs from all angles. The keystone is the Exceptional Family Member Program (**EFMP**).

EFMP was given a big boost by a former commandant of the Marine

Corps, General James Jones, whose son had Down syndrome. Throughout his military career in the 1960s and '70s, he thought he had to hide that fact because he felt it might hurt his career prospects. When he joined the military leadership, he threw his support behind the effort so that the needs of military families are met, and so no service member's career may be hurt in the process.

Military service members are required by regulations to enroll their family member in EFMP via DEERS if a health care provider gives them that designation. When a family member is given the EFMP designation by a doctor, the first door that opens is the array of medical benefits that become available and paid for by Tricare. Some medical conditions, such as autism, require extra approval for the Extended Care Health Option (**ECHO**). ECHO covers additional costs not normally covered by Tricare, but still there are some fees.

According to Tricare, the monthly cost share is only one fee per sponsor, not per ECHO beneficiary. You pay only the cost share if you used ECHO benefits during that calendar month.

Pay Grade	Monthly Cost Share
E-1 to E-5	$25
E-6	$30
E-7, O-1	$35
E-8, O-2	$40
E-9, W-1, W-2, O-3	$45
W-3, W-4, O-4	$50
W-5, O-5	$65
O-6	$75
O-7	$100
O-8	$150
O-9	$200
0–10	$250

After you pay the monthly cost share, Tricare will pay up to $2,500 per calendar month for each ECHO-registered beneficiary for authorized ECHO benefits (the limit on ECHO Home Health Care benefits is separate; see below). If an ECHO beneficiary's costs exceed $2,500 in a calendar month, you are responsible for paying the additional costs.

Many families use EFMP and ECHO for developmental issues related to their children, including special education programs—and they can be exceptionally good. In my son's case, ECHO covered the majority of costs for behavioral therapy in a school setting because he simply could not handle being in a traditional school. ECHO also covers training, rehabilitation, assistive technology devices, and even institutional home and respite care. It is a truly exceptional benefit for many military families.

EFMP provides you with a Specialized Care Organization Record (**SCOR**) to track a special needs child's medicines, exams, and treatments. Because health care records occasionally get lost, especially during relocation, and because there is a high turnover in health professionals, the SCOR is an extremely useful tool in getting continuous services from medical and other providers.

EFMP staff are primarily located at MTFs, and they not only help you navigate your benefits but also have tremendous insider knowledge of the programs that work. ECHO case managers are a subset of folks within the EFMP staff but located at Tricare offices. EFMP staff also maintain social networks of parents and caregivers who are going through the same thing you are. Equally important, they and military families continue to work together to improve services and health coverage to family members with special needs. A recent example is the creation of the Autism Services Demonstration project, which enhances access to services.

There are EFMP specialists in personnel commands and family support offices, depending on the military branch and location. These good folks are here to help you do things such as find suitable housing and services.

Because the best medical care and services for exceptional family members are found at MTFs, the EFMP designation *must* be factored in during the personnel assignment process. Simply put, the service member cannot be assigned to a duty station where care is not available to the family member or is difficult to obtain. Additionally, the service member receives priority placement in locations where care is available. This can be waived in special circumstances, but not often. Also, this does not mean the service member will not deploy. It simply means he likely will be stationed in a major CONUS metropolitan area from which he will deploy. Don't think you can use EFMP status to get out of deployment.

Your EFMP Category established by your doctor determines your limitations on duty stations. While the Army vaguely says it will consider EFMP status when determining a duty station, other services are more specific:*

CATEGORY 1: Needs of the family member do not generally limit duty stations.

CATEGORY 2: Pinpoint assignments INCONUS (in the continental United States) or OCONUS (outside the continental United States) (to make sure services are available).

CATEGORY 3: No overseas assignment for your family member is authorized unless appropriate medical and/or educational services are available. However, the service member may still be assigned an unaccompanied tour.

CATEGORY 4: Major medical areas INCONUS only. However, the service member may still be deployed or sent on an unaccompanied tour. Category 4 families are given priority-housing assignment, which defined, is the first available house that meets the needs of the Category 4 Exceptional Family Member.

CATEGORY 5 (Navy only): Allows service member to "homestead" their entire career in an area with an MTF. He is not exempt from deployments or unaccompanied tours, but his family will stay put.

CATEGORY P or 6: Exceptional Family Members who have submitted their application and are awaiting a category to be assigned. Emergency measures may be taken if needed and agreed upon by medical provider and personnel office.

Tricare Regions and Contact Information

Tricare Region North
Health Net Federal Services, LLC
1-877-TRICARE (1-877-874-2273)
1-800-555-2605 (*Tricare Reserve Select*)
www.healthnetfederalservices.com

---

*Sources include Army Regulation 608–75, the Military HOMEfront, and the MCCS websites.

Tricare Region South
Humana Military Healthcare Services, Inc.
1-800-444-5445
1-877-298-3408 (*National Guard and Reserve*)
1-877-249-9179 (*active duty programs*)
www.humana_military.com

Tricare Region West
TriWest Healthcare Alliance Corp.
1-888-TRIWEST (1-888-874-9378)
www.triwest.com

Tricare Pharmacy Options
www.tricare.mil/pharmacy
Mail Order Pharmacy
1-866-DoD-TMOP (1-866-363-8667)
Member Choice Center (MCC)
1-877-363-1433
www.tricare.mil/pharmacy
Tricare Network Retail Pharmacy (to find an authorized pharmacy)
1-866-DoD-TRRX (1-866-363-8779)
www.tricare.mil/pharmacy

Tricare Dental Program
United Concordia Companies, Inc.
1-800-866-8499
www.Tricaredentalprogram.com

Tri-Service Remote Dental Program
Military Medical Support Office
1-888-MHS-MMSO (1-888-647-6676)
mmso.med.navy.mil

Mail   Tricare Area Office, Tricare Europe
        Unit 10310
        APO AE 09136-0130

Phone   Toll-free: 1-888-777-8343
         011-49-6302-67-7432
         DSN: 496-7432
Fax   011-49-6302-67-6374
         DSN Fax: 496-6374
E-mail   teurope@europe.tricare.osd.mil

Mail   Director, Tricare Area Office, Latin America and Canada
         TAO-LAC, Bldg. 38716, 38th Alley
         Fort Gordon, GA 30905-5650
Phone   Toll-free: 1-888-777-8343
         1-706-787-2424
         DSN: 773-2424
Fax   1-706-787-3024
E-mail   taolac@tma.osd.mil

Mail   Tricare Area Office, Pacific NH Okinawa
         PSC 482, Box 2749
         FPO AP 96362
Phone   Toll-free: 1-888-777-8343
         011-81-6117-43-2036
         DSN: 643-2036
         Remote sites: 011-65-6-338-9277
Fax   011-81-611-743-2037
         DSN Fax: 643-2037
E-mail   tpao.csc@med.navy.mil

Overseas Claims Information
*(including pharmacy, except for Guam, Puerto Rico,
and the U.S. Virgin Islands only)*
Wisconsin Physicians Service
1-608-301-2310 or 1-608-301-2311
www.tricare4u.com

Dental Care

Service members receive free dental care through military dentists, and they are required to have regularly scheduled appointments. For families, inexpensive dental insurance using civilian dentists is offered by the military through a contractor, United Concordia (www.ucci.com).

There are two plans you can purchase. The single-member plan covers only one dependent and costs just $11.58 per month (per 2009 rates). The family plan covers multiple family members and costs just $28.95 per month. The maximum United Concordia will spend on any enrollee in any fiscal year is $1,200, although certain preventative and diagnostic treatments are not applied against that maximum. Additionally, there is a $1,500 lifetime cap on orthodontia for each enrollee.

Your service member will sign you up for coverage in the Tricare Dental Program (TDP—the overarching government authority) and arrange your monthly payment to be taken by allotment directly from your service member's pay.

———— *Did You Know?* ————

Be aware that there are delays between signing up and actually receiving dental coverage, so don't wait to enroll. You don't want to spend a month in agony with a chipped tooth before you can see a dentist, and you may not receive coverage at that point anyway, since the incident happened before you were covered.

The Least You Need to Know

> Military doctors are trained in regular medical schools, but they have special expertise in military-specific needs, such as tropical diseases and biological and chemical warfare.
> Tricare is just like a regular HMO. You have to work the system to reap the benefits, and that means working with your doctor to get the care you need covered by insurance.

CHAPTER 9

Relocation and Housing

"**R**elocation" is a scary word for many new military wives and women, but it sometimes means adventure for the more experienced. The first move is always the most difficult because of the stress of moving and learning your way through the bureaucratic process. Every move after that gets easier, and believe it or not, many families turn relocation into a family vacation. If you learn the system and follow the tips and tricks of your fellow wives, you, too, can make relocation easy and even fun.

As stated earlier, the frequency and distance of any relocation depends on your service member's career. I'd estimate that 80 percent of military families can predict where they'll be stationed next. For the 20 percent who can't, either they weren't paying attention to the duty stations at stake or the system had a last-minute duty station that only your service member could fill. Of course, there also have been situations where the service member misled his spouse about available duty stations to follow his preferred career track, even though it meant living in a less preferable location. Many hard-core Marines, for example, would love to be stationed in bizarrely remote locations with great operational opportunities, such as Twentynine Palms, California, even though their families might go crazy from the heat and lack of civilization.

Whatever your situation, you and your service member should be

WAR STORIES

Turning Relocation into a Family Vacation

When my husband and I did our first move together from Washington, D.C., to San Diego, we saw it as a tremendous opportunity to spend 10 days together and see the country. With our two dogs in tow, we knew that our daily drive time would be limited and there would be no way to visit any indoor tourist attractions. We opted to spend the first day driving as far as possible just to get the trip moving. We ended up in Nashville and stayed at a La Quinta Inn near the airport with a huge field to play ball in. The next day, we detoured from the freeway and traveled the Natchez Trace and then west to Shiloh National Military Park. After spending several hours walking with the dogs through that historic landmark, we hit the back roads and drove over the Mississippi River, on into Little Rock, Arkansas.

The next morning we ate a southern-fried breakfast and headed west into the Ozark Mountains through more back roads, trying to see the legendary land of the Hatfields and McCoys. By Oklahoma City, we had picked up old Route 66 and then toured the famous sites along it, including Cadillac Ranch, and spent the night in Amarillo, Texas. The next day was a short drive to Albuquerque for a visit with old friends, followed by a detour through the old mining town and ski resort of Durango, Colorado, the Mesa Verde cliff dwellings (another national park), an Indian fry bread stand at Four Corners, and the Painted Desert of Arizona. After two nights with family, we completed our journey to San Diego with several days to spare.

We had so much fun, we're planning our next cross-country trip across the northern United States so we can see Yellowstone National Park, the site of Custer's Last Stand, Mount Rushmore, and other sites along the Lewis and Clark trail.

having lengthy discussions about your future at least six months before applying for duty stations, when your Job Guy begins to indicate which positions might be available. When it comes time for your service member to see the actual list of duty stations and select his top three or four choices, neither you nor he should be surprised, and he should be able to enter his choices by rote without having to check with you. This is important in case your service member is forced to negotiate with his Job Guy or with other service members competing for the same duty stations and cannot call you to discuss the options.

Moving Your Household Goods

All relocations are handled by your base Personal Property Office (**PPO**) of the Traffic Management Office (**TMO**). Either PPO or TMO may be referred to when base officials talk about who handles your move, so be aware of both acronyms. We'll use "TMO" when discussing this bureaucracy.

Before you freak out over the cost of movers and en route hotels, know that the military is required to pay for moving your family as well as your household goods.

For a Permanent Change of Station (**PCS**) move—typically referred to as "PCSing"—you have three choices on how to move your household goods: commercial movers hired by the military, a do-it-yourself or DITY move, or a combination of both, known as a partial DITY move. The first choice is the easiest. Professional movers pack all of your stuff and get it to you within a specific period of time, based on the distance between locations. Believe it or not, they are better than you at packing your wedding china, and they're required to unpack all your stuff upon arrival (although you must put it away). The military will pay for your move only up to a certain weight allowance, which is dependent on your pay grade. Although very few families exceed their weight allowance, it's worth it to throw a premove yard sale to avoid paying moving costs for anything above your weight allowance. According to the Department of Defense, a good way to estimate your total weight is to figure 1,000

2009 Table of Joint Federal Travel Regulations Weight Allowances
*Allowances. Except as provided in pars. U5315 and
U5330-A, authorized PCS weight allowances are:*

PCS & NTS Weight Allowances (Pounds)

	Grades 1 and 3, With Dependents	Grade 2, Without Dependents
Officer Personnel		
0–10 to 0–6	18,000	18,000
0–5/W-5	17,500	16,000
0–4/W-4	17,000	14,000
0–3/W-3	14,500	13,000
0–2/W-2	13,500	12,500
0–1/W-1/Service Academy Graduates	12,000	10,000
Enlisted Personnel		
E-9	15,000	13,000
E-8	14,000	12,000
E-7	13,000	11,000
E-6	11,000	8,000
E-5	9,000	7,000
E-4	8,000	7,000
E-3 to E-1	8,000	5,000
Aviation Cadets	8.000	7,000

Grade 1 includes a Uniformed Service regular and Reserve Component member, and an officer holding a temporary commission in the U.S. Army or U.S. Air Force.

Source: Joint Federal Track Regulations.

pounds per room (not including bathrooms), then add that to the estimated weight of appliances and other large items you plan to move.

It is also important to note that the military will not ship any automobiles if you are moving within CONUS (the continental United States), and it will ship only one car if you are moving overseas. As a result, most families relocate within CONUS using two cars. And that makes a DITY or partial DITY more plausible—if not profitable—for families who don't have a lot of furniture to move.

DITY moves are not for the faint of heart or those who tend to be disorganized. Basically, the government estimates its cost to move your household goods, and then pays you 95 percent of that cost to move it yourself. You can get 65 percent of the money in advance so that expenses such as a rental truck and packing materials don't come out of your pocket. The government's allocation is based on the weight of your household goods, not to exceed your weight allowance. Whether you use your car or a rental truck, you will be expected to weigh your empty vehicle in advance and then again when full at an official truck-weighing station to determine the weight of your household goods. Those are the same weigh stations you see on the side of the highway with hordes of Mack trucks. The weight cannot include a car in tow. Your TMO counselor will give you more specific details on what is required to certify your weight, but there are definitely a couple of hoops to jump through.

Did You Know?

If you are relocating and hope to move into base housing, plan to live in temporary civilian lodging first. It may take several months before your number comes up on the base housing waiting list. In the meantime, you can either move twice (the second time at your expense) or keep your stuff in storage.

Be careful: If you overestimate the weight during counseling and receive an advance, and then find out you have less weight when you measure it at the truck-weighing station, you will have to pay back the extra amount. Also, be sure to get approval from TMO for a DITY move or you might not get paid or even reimbursed for your expenses. TMO also strongly recommends getting insurance for your rental truck and household goods during shipment. And storage of your DITY-moved goods at your destination may increase your costs; since the government doesn't like to deal with DITY storage, it will reimburse you only for what they

DLA Rates for 2009

Effective January 1, 2009

Grade	Without-Dependent Rate	With-Dependent Rate
O-10	$3,318.33	$4,084.83
O-9	$3,318.33	$4,084.83
O-8	$3,318.33	$4,084.83
O-7	$3,318.33	$4,084.83
O-6	$3,044.30	$3,678.02
O-5	$2,932.06	$3,545.24
O-4	$2,717.18	$3,125.18
O-3	$2,177.60	$2,585.57
O-2	$1,727.36	$2,207.77
O-1	$1,454.55	$1,973.62
O-3E	$2,351.42	$2,778.73
O-2E	$1,998.96	$2,507.16
O-1E	$1,718.91	$2,316.41
W-5	$2,760.62	$3,016.54
W-4	$2,451.60	$2,765.48
W-3	$2,060.52	$2,533.70
W-2	$1,829.98	$2,330.91
W-1	$1,531.80	$2,015.87
E-9	$2,013.46	$2,654.41
E-8	$1,848.07	$2,446.80
E-7	$1,578.89	$2,271.76
E-6	$1,429.19	$2,099.14
E-5	$1,318.15	$1,887.89
E-4	$1,146.73	$1,887.89
E-3	$1,125.01	$1,887.89
E-2	$913.77	$1,887.89
E-1	$814.81	$1,887.89

Source: Per Diem Committee.

would pay at a government facility and does not reimburse for damage that occurs during a DITY storage.

Again, talk to TMO or the relocation counselor at your base Family Support Center to help determine whether a commercial or a DITY move—or some combination—is right for you. Equally important, before you sign up for a DITY move, be sure to call around to find the best price on rental trucks and insurance. You'll find that one-way rentals are astoundingly expensive, and a DITY move may not be as profitable as you think.

Reimbursement for Your Travel

The military recognizes that it costs a lot of money to move your family to your new home, so it offers several types of reimbursement. The biggest chunk of change will come from Dislocation Allowance (**DLA**) to cover the cost of, well, "dislocation" from your current home. Be sure to have your service member ask your relocation counselor or personnel office (such as the Navy's Personnel Support Detachment or **PSD**) for the latest rates, since they change from year to year.

Did You Know?

The government will insist that you pay for relocation expenses on the government-issued credit card as much as possible. As explained in chapter 7, "Personal Finances—Military Style," be very careful to ensure that every cent of your statement is paid in full, and you do not use it for personal expenses unrelated to your PCS, or you may be reported to your command.

Although DLA is generally paid 10 days in advance, your DLA may not show up as soon as you need it to begin covering moving expenses. Be sure to nag your service member to press his command admin to pay

WAR STORIES

We recently completed our ninth move in 10 years, but I found it the hardest because we have two small children. My immediate concerns were the children getting underfoot of the movers, getting into stuff, or putting the inevitable floor debris into their mouths. So my husband and I chose to travel together to reach his parents' home, and then he stayed for a few days while I traveled on to meet the movers and unpack.

I have not come across a more challenging moving crew. Instead of the promised 7:00 A.M. arrival, they showed up at 11:00 A.M. on what forecasters later named the hottest day of the summer. From the beginning, I told them we would have the entire house unpacked and all boxes gone by the end of the day. I gave them doughnuts while I showed them where everything would go, pointed out a bevy of beverages from which they could avail themselves, and got them to work.

That's when the backlash began. First, the driver told me he was on disability and could not lift heavy objects. The other movers grumbled with resentment, so I put the driver to work unloading clothes. "You want me to go through your underwear and everything?" exclaimed the driver. "Yes," I responded with confidence and shooed him off. The other movers smirked and seemed a bit more motivated.

I made an effort to smile, get to know their names, and ask about their families. Within an hour, they wanted a cigarette break but claimed they were out of cigarettes. If they left to get cigarettes, I knew it would be hours before they returned. Since it was lunchtime anyway, I offered to get cigarettes and the lunch of their choice. Their faces brightened. I returned within 15 minutes to find the stereo unpacked. As I handed out lunch, I asked them to turn on the radio station of their choice. Now they were jammin'!

The driver continued to balk, but I put him to work assembling beds and other doable tasks. Every time the movers put down stacked items meant for drawers or cabinets, I swept around to put them away and clear counter space for more. They groaned with the knowledge that I had done this before, but they finally succumbed to just getting it done right.

At 10:00 P.M., the movers drove away with all but five boxes unpacked. The kitchen items were disorganized but put away in cabinets and drawers, and relatively functional. Two days later, my husband walked into a fully unpacked and vacuumed house, with groceries in the fridge. He only needed to help me put pictures on the wall. My kids ate a good meal and slept soundly in rooms that felt like home. It was exhausting, but it helped settle my family in a very satisfying way.

his DLA as soon as possible. The worst-case scenario is that it arrives long after you've maxed out your credit cards with hotel and gas station bills.

In the same lump sum payment with DLA, you will typically receive your Travel Allowance (although you can receive it after you arrive if you don't ask for it early). This is intended to cover your actual travel and food expenses during the trip, and the combination of those items cannot exceed $109 per day (in 2009 rates within CONUS). It is a combination of the service member's Personal Travel Allowance (24 cents per mile plus flat per diem of $50). The Travel Allowance also authorizes a per diem of $72 for dependents ages 12 and older and a flat rate of $48 per day for ages 11 and under. Mileage and travel time between your current home and your new home have already been estimated by the Department of Defense, so check with your relocation counselor or PSD to see how much you'll receive or visit the Per Diem Committee website for their extensive calculators at perdiem.hqda.pentagon.mil/perdiem/.

If you are relocating overseas, your personnel office will give your command admin a packet of information and forms to fill out with you, including preferences for travel, which will dictate your DLA and travel pay. Passport forms and other technical problems also will be covered. Never fear! Your command admin will guide you through and help make travel arrangements within your budget, probably via a space-available flight on a military transport plane. For those receiving last-minute orders overseas, you can quickly apply online at the State Department's

Personally Procured Move Claim Estimate

2009-01-26	Estimate Date
3 Weeks	Estimated Processing Time
$3,970.62	Member Entitlement
$992.66	Tax
$2,977.96	Net Member Entitlement
$2,382.37	Available Advance

Valid **empty and full vehicle weight tickets must be submitted** to determine actual weight of household goods. Move weight cannot exceed authorized weight.

The **tax amount can be reduced** by providing valid receipts for allowable deductions such as the cost of a rental vehicle, packing materials, moving aids, tolls, and gasoline.

Please note that this estimate uses the 60 percent rate for calculating the available advance. This rate is used by all military branches except for the Marine Corps, which uses a 50 percent rate.

This estimate is based on the following values:

Personally Procured Move Calculator

887	Miles
9,000	Estimated Pounds
11,000	Authorized Pounds
E-6	Pay Grade
YES	Dependents
NOV 08–APR 09	Move Month
w08	Volume
PERMANENT	Move Type
inter	Trans Type
FL	Origination State
PENSACOLA	City
ESCAMBIA	County
VA	Destination State
CHESAPEAKE	City
CHESAPEAKE	County
46.44	Net Rate

9,000	Net Weight
$4,179.60	Government Cost
CONT	GBLOC
A	Schedule
3	Section Number
w05	Source
120.00	Rate Percent
95.00	Entitlement Percent
60.00	Advance Percent
25.00	Tax Rate
27.40	Mileage Rate
9,000	Mileage Weight
11.30	Packing Rate
9,000	Packing Weight

Source: *Fleet & Industrial Supply Team Household Goods Audit Team Division (pptas
.ahf.nmci.navy.mil/).*

website for a no-fee passport and receive it in as quickly as 10 days. That
will at least allow you to PCS to the overseas base. If you wish to travel
beyond the military base (and you will), then you still need to apply for
a tourist visa. Again, the State Department website moves pretty quickly
(typically within 10 days), or go to a local post office and pay for expedited service (about $100).

Temporary Lodging Expenses (**TLE**) is a little-known authorized pay
in addition to your Travel and Dislocation Allowances. It's little known
because you have to request it from your command admin, and the paperwork is a bit complicated.

TLE is intended to briefly cover your lodging expenses once you arrive at your duty station but before you settle into a home. You cannot be
paid TLE if you do your house hunting in advance of your PCS. You can
receive this pay for up to 10 days if your new duty station is CONUS, five
days if you are headed overseas. If you are stuck overseas with no housing, you receive a Temporary Lodging Allowance or **TLA** and/or placed
in furnished temporary housing on base. Do not fear! I have never once
heard of any military family finding themselves stuck overseas with no-

where to live. The relocation folks are good at this, so work with them. You should arrange for TLE in advance instead of being reimbursed on arrival. Receipts must be provided either way, and your mileage must be calculated, which is why most people don't bother with TLE. Without receipts, the military will force you to pay back TLE by withholding your service member's pay. In addition, you cannot receive TLE for your first or your last PCS. The government figures it doesn't owe you for that. Yet TLE can add up quickly, so I recommend sticking a manila envelope in your travel bag and shoving in every receipt acquired during your trip.

Did You Know?

Security deposits on utilities can get expensive! You may be able to avoid them by asking your current utility company to send you letters of reference for your new utility company to review when setting up an account.

Finally, the military will give you an advance on your Basic Allowance for Housing (BAH) as a loan to cover the costs of moving in, such as deposits on a new apartment and utilities (not government housing). You then pay back this interest-free loan over 12 months through an allotment. See your command admin for more information. Our advice is to get advance BAH to cover deposits on your new location, but pay it back immediately upon receiving your security deposits back from the old location.

House-Hunting Leave

According to DoD regulations, your service member is authorized to take up to 10 days of house-hunting leave, and even more for a PCS overseas. This time off is in addition to regular vacation and travel time between bases. However, not all commands authorize house-hunting leave if things are too hectic to allow time off, so be sure to have your service member check with his new command. Sometimes it is better to take house-hunting leave a few months before moving, to secure a place to live immediately upon arrival. In such cases, time will be taken away from and must be authorized by the old command. More frequently, a new command will allow the service member to tack on the 10 days of house-hunting leave to his travel time, even if he has already found a place to live.

Please note that if you opt to house-hunt upon arrival at your new CONUS duty station, you can receive the TLE allowance—but not if you opt to house-hunt before you relocate. You will have to bear the expenses of travel and lodging. Overseas house hunting is different, and it is possible to receive five days of TLE for it.

————————— *Did You Know?* —————————

Even though most base legal offices can get you a POA within 10 minutes without an appointment, relying on your service member to deal with TMO is not a bad idea, even if you are a complete control freak. Surprisingly, there are only about two forms to fill out, both of which require his signature anyway, and the only thing TMO wants to know is when you want your stuff packed up and when you want it delivered. TMO may make your service member sit through a mind-numbing one-hour class on how to move, but he's used to these types of lectures by now, and some of the information can be quite helpful.

The major reason for not house hunting in advance is that travel expenses may not be covered by TLE, even overseas. For many spouses PCSing within CONUS, however, having control of where you live and advance planning are worth spending a weekend and a couple of hundred dollars to house-hunt. When moving overseas, no one house-hunts in advance. It's nearly impossible, expensive, and most people live in base housing anyway, so it all depends on what is available the moment you arrive. Overseas moves are very stressful for this reason, but you have no choice but to trust the hundreds of thousands of military families who have done this before you. It will turn out just fine.

This is admittedly all very confusing. If I am boring you by repeating the need to visit your relocation counselor, personnel office, and TMO, be assured that they can tie up all of the above details into one basic estimate for your total cost of moving and reimbursement. You'll feel much more in control of your finances—and moving options—when you receive your individualized relocation estimates.

The Logistical Process of Moving with the Military

Legally speaking, spouses are not authorized to work with TMO to move household goods unless you have a specific Power of Attorney (**POA**) from the base legal office. TMO will tell you that's because the military is really paying for the service member's move, not yours, even if 95 percent of the "household goods" is your stuff. Yes, you are chopped liver in their eyes.

——————————— *Did You Know?* ———————————

Most relocations take place in December or late spring/early summer, so you want to beat the stampede to visit TMO, your relocation counselor, and command admin and schedule your move as soon as you receive orders.

The real story, however, is that a handful of military wives took advantage of TMO in the past to move their household goods to a new location when the service member had no orders to move or was moving to a different location. In other words, these ladies got TMO to help them leave their husbands. How they got away with it, I don't know, because TMO requires you to show proof of orders to relocate before they'll even discuss relocation with you. And you can't relocate to a household that is more than 50 miles from your new command. Even so, these ladies' stories made for terrific mythology within the TMO bureaucracy, and now the rest of us are forced to rely on our service member or get a POA.

Within a week or so of submitting the requisite paperwork and proof of orders to TMO, you should receive a response telling you which moving company has been hired, when they will arrive, and approximately when they will deliver your stuff at your new location. The sooner you submit this paperwork and get the process going, the more likely you will be moved on the preferred dates you indicated.

Storage

The military generally does not like to deal with storage, but you are entitled to up to 90 days of temporary storage at origin, en route, or at the final destination during any PCS move. Extensions are possible, as is permanent storage in certain circumstances, so talk to your TMO counselor.

You also can have movers pick up your household goods from storage, but TMO warns that you are required to meet the movers at the storage facility and unpack your goods so they can repack and load them professionally.

Shipping Your Cars

Service members are currently entitled to have only one car (referred to as a Personally Owned Vehicle or **POV**) shipped if they are moving overseas. The military will not ship cars for a move within CONUS. There is some discussion of changing this policy because of the dangerousness of families driving two cars cross-country, and to reflect the needs of modern families. The military will ship motorcycles as part of your household weight allowance.

For overseas relocation, many families opt not to ship their car because (1) you must first drop it off at a military car-shipment port, which may be hundreds of miles away; (2) it takes forever (90 days) for the vehicle to arrive; (3) American cars often are not permitted to operate in the destination country or at least do not fit in well; and (4) the military will pay to store your vehicle while you are away. SUVs are particularly difficult to drive on the narrow roads of many foreign countries. Also, in many foreign countries cars are driven on the left-hand side of the road, instead of the right-hand side, as in America. For this reason, American cars with the driver's seat on the left side make it confusing and even dangerous to drive in other countries. Better to arrive, drive a rental car for a bit to familiarize yourself, and then buy a car locally. You can have it shipped back to the United States upon your return if you wish, but many families just sell it to the next incoming military family.

For moves within CONUS, some families opt to have their vehicle shipped at their own expense. The cost is typically around $1,500 for a cross-country move, and you can receive your car usually within 15 days or so. Obviously, this is an additional expense, but it is an alternative for families who worry about both parents driving simultaneously across country or who want to turn their trip into a family vacation. If you have a medical voucher from your doctor, it may be possible to get the military to pay for shipment of one vehicle within CONUS.

Did You Know?

Unless you have a reason to be concerned about both adults driving, I recommend getting a cheap walkie-talkie system and driving both cars. You'll save a ton of money and still be able to chatter all the way.

Shipping a Mobile Home

A mobile home may be shipped at government expense if you are PCSing within CONUS or overseas, as long as you plan to use it as a residence. Temporary storage (90 days) is approved but may not be available in your location. This is one time when it may pay for you to do a DITY move of your home instead of having the government move your home for you. Again, check with PPO regarding your entitlements.

Shipping Firearms

The shipment of firearms is probably the last thing you're concerned about during your move, but your service member probably owns at least one and there are regulations involved. If the movers will not pack them for you or if you are worried they will be stolen, you may have to travel with your firearms in your baggage. That means you must pack them appropriately (i.e., dismantled and unloaded) and carry your registration with you. It is also important to have your military I.D. and orders in hand because some states and countries prohibit some types of firearms unless owned by a military service member. When traveling with firearms to and from overseas locales, be sure to declare them on your customs forms to prevent an international incident. It would not be pleasant for friends and family to see your face on CNN as a detained alleged terrorist.

Relocating Pets

The first thing you need to relocate your pet is a recent health certificate (within 20 days of travel) from your current veterinarian stating that your pet is healthy and up to date on its vaccinations. While this is not as critical when moving within CONUS, it is critical when moving overseas. Because of the incidence of rabies within the United States, many foreign countries and the state of Hawaii require certification of rabies vaccination and may still quarantine your pet for 30 days or longer. Most countries also charge a pet entrance fee and may restrict certain exotic pets and dog breeds, namely pit bull terriers. For details on your destination, visit the Military HOMEfront website to see what regulations the country has on your pet.

When traveling with pets within CONUS, most families carry the pet in the car using a pet carrier and make plenty of bathroom stops. Be sure to make your travel plans in advance, as most hotels do not accept pets. The only nationwide exception I am aware of is La Quinta Inns (1-800-531-5900), which accept up to two well-behaved pets up to 40 pounds at all their locations. (God bless them!)

It may sound inhumane, but some pet owners opt to give their pets light sleeping pills before traveling with them on a plane, or Dramamine if traveling by car. It spares the pet (and you) the stress of travel. Talk to your vet before taking chances with your pet's medications.

When relocating pets overseas, you should be able to fly them with you whether you are traveling by commercial or military aircraft. However, be sure to check the rules before assuming your pets are okay to go. Most important, let your travel planner know that you have pets when scheduling your family's overseas travel. They will help arrange for your pets to travel with you. You also can check with commercial airlines, and particularly Delta, to see what they offer for a fee. Just be cautious when shipping a pet during hot or cold weather.

If your pet cannot travel overseas with you, consider foster care with NetPets.org. Their mission is simply to help relocating military families take care of their pets. There is no reason to abandon your pet when such a great resource is available.

Traveling Overseas

Besides the issue of temporary lodging, the main thing to know about traveling overseas is that it just takes longer to receive your household goods. For that reason, the military typically pays for a temporary rental car and permits a small shipment of "unaccompanied baggage" (i.e., stuff you will need immediately upon arrival while waiting for your main shipment of household goods). Unaccompanied baggage is packed and shipped separately from your household goods and usually includes items such as kitchen utensils and dishes, daily-use linens, and baby cribs. You may take only 25 percent of your weight allowance for your unaccompanied baggage, so choose wisely and assume you will live for two months without the remaining 75 percent of your stuff.

Moving Out

If you plan to have the military handle your move, the moving company will probably call you to set up a premove meeting, in which they review your household to get an idea of how much weight and bulk they will have to pack. They have no restrictions on dealing with spouses, so now you can take back control of your move. This is a good opportunity to assess the professionalism of your mover, get contact phone and cell phone numbers, and find out how long the process will take. If you have any concerns about your mover, or hear something bad through the grapevine, call TMO immediately and ask to be assigned to a different company. You may not be moved on the dates you preferred, and the TMO bureaucrat may give you a bit of a hassle, but at least your stuff will arrive intact. The military gives most movers up to two days to pack your house, one day for packing and one day for loading, and most movers will use all of that time to be paid the highest rate.

The week before your move, you will start to get anxious and try to prepack things. Don't. Instead, try to focus your energy on saying goodbye to old friends. The two to three days before your move, however, there are several things you can do to get organized for the big day:

> ⟩ If moving overseas, separate your unaccompanied baggage from your main shipment of household goods. You may take only 25 percent of your total weight allowance as unaccompanied baggage.
> ⟩ Give away your household plants to friends and neighbors, and wash out any good pots you wish to keep.

> Disconnect all household appliances you intend to ship, and defrost the refrigerator at least 24 hours in advance.

> If shipping machines such as a motorcycle or a lawn mower, remove any gasoline or oil from the engine.

> Clean out your garage of anything the movers are unlikely to pack and that you probably won't use in the future, such as paint, aerosols, and cleansers.

> Back up important files on your computer, and plan to take it with you.

> Record the serial numbers and, if possible, take photos of any expensive electronic equipment or furniture. This prevents a disreputable mover from attempting to deliver a 20-year-old clunker TV instead of the brand-new flat-screen you actually own.

> Separate the service member's and your professional goods, such as books or equipment, from the rest of the household. The movers should weigh them separately because they will not count against your weight allowance (up to a point).

> Dismantle anything with electrical cords, such as computers, televisions, and stereos.

> Purchase food and drinks for yourself and the movers, such as sodas, doughnuts, and granola bars. Plan to buy your movers lunch. Bribery and goodwill are everything to your movers!

> Arrange for day care and pet care if possible. Kids and pets tend to get in the way and create safety hazards, and just watching the move will unnecessarily stress them out.

> Empty your trash can and put out a large trash bag with a big sign that says TRASH. Otherwise the movers will pack your full trash can, which you will discover weeks later when you unpack.

> If you are driving two cars, invest in walkie-talkies for the trip. It makes driving safer and more fun.

> Consider investing in an overhead travel compartment that is secured on top of your car. It clears out space inside the car, making travel safer and more comfortable, and you'll use it for years to come.

You will also need to set aside items you want to take with your family while you travel. I strongly recommend putting all of these items in your car the night before to ensure that they fit reasonably comfortably and so the movers don't accidentally pack them. These items include:

> Packed suitcases for the entire family.
> Important files, such as your service member's orders and service records, the household inventory list the movers will provide you, serial numbers and photos of any expensive equipment and furniture, car ownership and insurance papers, and Tricare insurance cards and phone numbers. You also should include the backed-up files from your computer.
> Expensive jewelry and other family heirlooms. Pack these at the bottom of your car where gas station thieves cannot quickly get to them.
> Travel toys for the kids.
> Snack foods for the trip.
> Paper plates, cups, and plastic utensils to use while living in an empty house. You may be too tired or forget to buy them when you arrive. Later on, this will save money and calories from eating out.
> Extra bath towels.
> Blankets and pillows to sleep on after the movers pack your bed and in case you have a few nights in your new home before they arrive.
> A small tool kit containing duct tape, a hammer, a four-headed screwdriver, scissors, and pliers.
> A laundry basket in which you will ultimately place all items the movers cannot pack, such as detergents, cosmetics, and aerosols. These items cost a lot when added together, and you'll need these anyway when you arrive at your new location and have an amazing urge to clean. Include in the laundry basket several rolls of toilet paper and paper towels because you'll be too tired to do a grocery run when you arrive. You can place the extra towels over the basket to keep things cool and prevent spills.
> Pet needs.
> Your walkie-talkies and cell phones.

If you plan to do a DITY or partial DITY move, you obviously want to call around to find the best price on a rental truck, assuming you need one. Be sure to do that months in advance to avoid the relocation stampede and ensure that you get access to a truck when you need it. Otherwise you are solely responsible for getting your stuff to the new location, and the military will accept no excuses for arriving late.

The anticipation of moving day is often worse than moving day itself. If professional movers are handling your move, you want to set aside a book to read or change-of-address cards to write because you'll have hours with nothing to do. Not only do you not have to pack anything, they won't allow you to for liability reasons!

Better yet, spend your time paying close attention to the Household Goods Descriptive Inventory list. The mover will tag every box or piece of furniture with a small sticker with a number on it. The mover in chief will subsequently record the tag number and the box's contents on the inventory list as it is being loaded onto the truck. It's important that every item is accounted for, because your stuff will be placed on a truck with at least one other shipment of household goods, and then it may be shipped, stored, and handled multiple times by the movers before arriving at the final destination. I don't care what TMO or the movers say: Your stuff will be double- or triple-handled by your destination. That means it will be loaded onto a moving truck, unloaded into a local storage unit, reloaded onto another truck for travel, unloaded at a second storage unit in your new hometown, and finally reloaded and delivered at your new doorstep. If you don't pay attention to the inventory list at both ends of your move, you increase the chance of boxes and furniture getting lost or stolen.

Did You Know?

Serious control freaks who are worried about losing their stuff go so far as to print out their own paper labels with their family's name and contact information and place one on each item. This way, other families who have received a stray box can call you and have it shipped.

Your moving day will start with the movers arriving to pack everything in boxes. They write the items contained on the outside of the boxes, and you should make absolutely sure the box does, in fact, contain what it says. Otherwise, the "pillows" box that contains your stereo will get tossed around. Or less reputable movers may deliberately mislabel boxes in the hope you won't care about that missing "pillows" box when you are too tired to unpack and verify. The moving crew chief will mark each box, its items, and their estimated weight (to make sure you don't go over your weight allowance) on the Household Goods Descriptive Inventory, a.k.a. DD Form 619.

Did You Know?

Superefficient control freaks label all their storage cabinets and drawers with Post-it notes in advance so movers themselves can place every item exactly where it needs to go.

Once the packing is done, the movers will take all of the boxes and furniture to the truck. At this point you need to park yourself at your front door with DD Form 619. They will call out their box numbers as they walk out the door, and you will check off each number on the list. Do not get distracted, and monitor every item! This is when most stuff gets stolen. For example, a mover might stroll out with a dolly carrying five boxes but call out only four numbers. That's because he is taking box five to his car and hoping you won't notice.

When everything is in the truck, the crew chief will give you three copies of DD Form 619 and ask you to sign them as verification that everything was packed correctly during the pack-out. Then you will be given the Government Bill of Lading describing approximately when the shipment will arrive at its destination and who your point of contact is.

If you're doing a DITY move, plan for some serious physical labor, and take time-outs to reenergize with food and rest.

Either way, expect to be exhausted and without a television or bed the night after moving day. If you're lucky, the movers may finish early and you can start your trip to the new base. More likely, however, you're better off enjoying an easygoing evening at your favorite restaurant and going to bed early on your makeshift bed. You have a long trip ahead!

—————— *Did You Know?* ——————

I have found it helpful for my husband to disappear or go to work on moving-in day, especially when I was pregnant. I complained vociferously that my husband was forced to work by his evil new command, and woe was me to be left alone and pregnant to put away all our belongings. The movers felt sorry for me and made a better effort to do a good job unpacking.

The Big Trip

Traveling with the family can be really fun! You're done with your move and free of responsibilities, so why not enjoy the scenery together? Like any family vacation, the key is to recognize family preferences and plan ahead. For example, if you are traveling by car across the country with children and pets, try to plan one outdoor excursion each day. You'll get to stretch your legs and see America's great national parks. Having said that, after a week or two of traveling, you and your family will have had enough and want nothing more than to settle in and eat a home-cooked meal. Plan for these preferences—and for contingencies—to avoid excessive tension during your trip.

If you are traveling overseas, most of your trip will be planned through your command admin, relocation counselor, and TMO, so you shouldn't have too much to worry about other than marking off each item on your to-do checklist. Once you're on the plane, however, you're free to relax and dream about future adventures—so long as you've brought the requisite snacks and toys to keep you and your family occupied during the long flight.

Moving In

Once you and your family arrive at your new location, notify TMO of your arrival (they will give you the phone number) and expect to hang out in an empty house for a few days. Movers rarely arrive exactly when they plan to, but usually will show up a day or so later. Getting a cell phone number of the company and/or driver is the best way to keep track of your shipment and plan. In the meantime, use the time to clean, line shelves with contact paper, and figure out where you want to place furniture and storage.

Did You Know?

Whenever possible, opt for a "door-to-door" move and do not allow your household goods to be placed in storage. For starters, it better ensures that all of your stuff arrives intact because the movers aren't at a storage facility guessing which stuff is yours. Second, the extra moving increases the likelihood of damage. Third, you don't know what that storage facility looks like. When we relocated to Pensacola, Florida, my movers insisted on moving in three days after Hurricane Katrina. I will never forget the huge Florida roaches racing around my sofa as the movers were carrying it in.

Moving in is more intensive than moving out. At this point, your goal is to get settled in as soon as possible. Why? Your family will be absolutely sick of traveling, and it's amazing how the stress disappears once you've reestablished familiar surroundings. Also, at this point you will probably have used up your DLA funds and/or Travel Allowance, and eating out is getting very expensive, not to mention calorie-laden.

The biggest mistake military families make is to let the movers leave without unpacking, which the military is paying them to do. The family is then overwhelmed with rooms full of boxes, having no idea which box contains what (even though each box is marked by room) and no way to dispose of the boxes. My girlfriend Robyne spent two months unpacking when she fell for an old movers' trick. The movers harassed her about having to unpack, and then dumped a box of medicine on the floor, where it spilled on the carpet. Frustrated, Robyne ordered them to stop and waived her right to have them unpack.

Experienced military families can have nearly their entire household unpacked—including pictures on the walls—within four days. Do not use this as your yardstick for success, however, especially on your first move. Just understand that the key to getting unpacked is having an efficient system whereby the movers systematically unpack room by room. As they put something down, you or someone in your family needs to pick it up and put it away. You will know approximately where to put it because you've reviewed your house the night before and gotten a good idea of where things should go.

Don't worry about getting everything exactly right. You can rearrange things later, once you've had a chance to live in your new home and establish new routines. Far more important is clearing a space for the movers to unpack the next item, and the next. If they run out of space on the countertops or floor, the movers will claim they can no longer unpack and you will be left to fend for yourself.

What should my girlfriend Robyne have done after the unprofessional behavior of her movers? Insist that they clean up the mess and tell them you expect them to be more professional and careful. If that doesn't work, call TMO immediately to report the problem or, if it's after office hours, call the base Inspector General. Either one is required to come to your home immediately, referee the dispute, and make sure your household items are unpacked safely and professionally. Do not attempt to handle the situation yourself, and do not be intimidated by the movers or worry that they will harm your stuff. TMO's job is to make sure your rights to a professional move are not violated.

Of course, it does help to make friends with the movers. Again, you want to start moving-in day by introducing yourself, walking the movers through the house, and pointing out where you want things. Tell them outright that you expect everything to be unpacked by the end of the day, and then tell them where they can find food and drinks. Buy them lunch at midday and turn on the radio to a station they want to listen to. It makes them happy and the day goes faster.

The second biggest mistake military families make is not paying close attention when checking off the inventory list and filing claims for lost or damaged goods. Hopefully, you made sure on moving-out day that all of your boxes and furniture were appropriately tagged and listed on the inventory list. Now you will be asked to check off each item as it is unloaded from the truck. This is also a good time to direct movers as to what boxes go to which room. Again, park yourself at your front door, check off the numbers called out by the movers, and tell them where to place the box. Any items that do not arrive with your shipment or are damaged should be immediately recorded on the mover's paperwork for PPO, DD Form 1840, a pink copy of which you are entitled to receive. Simultaneously, ask the mover to simply check back at his warehouse for the stray item.

After you've signed DD Form 1840 acknowledging any lost or damaged items, the mover will send a copy to TMO, and you will have 70 days to report any additional lost or damaged items and nine months to file the completed claim. Be sure to report everything, because your homeowners or renters insurance will not pay for it. Some people buy private moving insurance, but the government now pays "Full Replacement Value" for lost or damaged items. Not only will you be reimbursed for the cost of your lost items, but also it helps TMO identify and impose quality controls on the movers they hire. Having photos and serial numbers on hand will help you process your claim more quickly and be reimbursed for the full amount.

Finally, the movers are required by the military to leave with any unpacked boxes. This is critical, because you may have difficulty disposing of them otherwise, and they take up a substantial amount of room. Many local garbage companies will not pick up boxes, and it is illegal to dump them in commercial Dumpsters.

Housing

You have two options for housing: government-subsidized housing, typically located on a military base, or regular civilian housing. "Housing" refers not only to homes but also to apartments, condos, mobile homes, and even houseboats. As a point of reference, within CONUS only 10 to 20 percent of military families live on base, while 80 to 90 percent live in civilian housing. Overseas, the reverse is more often the case.

The decision to live in base housing within CONUS is usually determined by personal preference, local cost of living, schools, the quality of housing, and the "pain in the butt" factor involved in dealing with base housing. First, personal preferences in housing often involve whether you don't mind living near your service member's colleagues and families, or whether you would prefer to put some distance between your family and your husband's work life. Sure, base housing is wonderfully Cleaveresque and safe (think kids playing baseball in the street), and it cuts down on your service member's commute time, but you also may have to put up with gossipy neighbors.

—————————— *Did You Know?* ——————————

Warning: Before signing up for a waiting list for a specific base neighborhood, be sure to check out the neighborhood, visit with the residents, and travel the distance between it and other important locations such as shopping, work, and day care. Some housing developments are so remote they don't have cell phone coverage. The residents will be happy to tell you everything you need to know because they wish they had had the same advice when they applied for housing. There's no sense in going through the bureaucracy and getting on a waiting list if you will ultimately refuse to live in a dumpy neighborhood.

Base housing also provides accommodations for family members with special needs, and EFMP families are prioritized on the housing list. By federal law, base housing is required to add wheelchair ramps or other necessary equipment. If you have special needs, be sure to research housing and floor plans, and notify the housing office well in advance. You may even be able to receive base housing if your service member is on an unaccompanied tour, and you may receive permission for extra space for a live-in aide. The second issue is that while those living in civilian housing receive a Basic Allowance for Housing (BAH), it may not be enough to cover rent in high-cost areas such as Washington, D.C. Many junior enlisted families opt for base housing because, although they lose their BAH payment, they often get a much bigger house and yard, and at no cost. The same size house in a civilian neighborhood would cost them hundreds of dollars extra out of their own pockets.

With regard to the third issue, I won't kid you that some of the current stock of base housing can be dilapidated and bug-infested. Fortunately, the government is completing a major campaign to rebuild base housing using private contractors, and overseas housing can be downright posh. This has significantly increased standards and quality for base housing.

You can see photos and floor plans of base housing developments on the Army Housing website at onestop.army.mil/. You need an AKO password to get even more detailed information on housing online, but you can even see Navy and DoD-wide housing availability. It also has a directory of housing offices. The Navy Housing website is similar, at www .housing.navy.mil/onestop/. The Defense Department also is creating a website for base housing and private housing at www.ahrn.com/. According to the promotional language, eventually military families will even be able to list their homes for rent or sale on this site.

Third is the critical issue of schools. Websites such as www.school matters.com and GreatSchools.com share reviews, ratings, and test score comparisons. However, there is no more valuable resource than parents who live there already. So be sure to ask the locals what the best schools are, and which ones to avoid.

Finally, there is no denying that dealing with the base Housing Office within CONUS can be a bureaucratic nightmare. To start, you must apply to be on a waiting list for housing, and you can only apply for housing that is designated for your pay grade, even if it is 30 miles from civilization. Even worse, Housing Offices will not allow you on the housing wait list until after you have PCS'd to the area. You should apply well in advance to receive a "control number" that will bump you up on this list when you arrive, but they won't confirm housing until you get there. Thus, even if you are living in Germany and can fax your orders to move to Fort Campbell, Kentucky, as proof that you will be relocating, the Fort Campbell Housing Office will not guarantee you housing. Amazingly, these very same bureaucrats are shocked—shocked!—when families show up on their doorstep and have no place to live. No, you are responsible for finding temporary housing until it's your turn to be assigned base housing. That could be months or even years depending on your base, and don't be surprised if your number on the wait list gets bumped by families with higher rank or special circumstances.

If you intend to pursue base housing, be sure to read any rental agreement you sign for temporary civilian housing carefully, because you could lose thousands if you attempt to break your rental agreement early. While most rentals near military bases have a "military contingency" clause, a closer inspection will show that you can break your rental agreement only if you have PCS orders to relocate more than 50 miles away. Getting into base housing does not count.

Did You Know?

If your service member deploys and you want to move back with your parents, you cannot get out of a rental agreement even with a military clause. That's because military clauses cover only a *permanent* change of station (PCS), not deployment or even temporary duty. It does cover Individual Augmentation and Unaccompanied Tours, both of which have permanent status. If you plan to move for any reason, it may be better to accept a shorter-term lease agreement than rely on the goodwill of the landlord. If the landlord balks at a legitimate permanent change, then call the JAG office or Housing office and let them fight it for you.

The base Housing Office will insist that you report to it even if you intend from the start to live in civilian housing. Well, no one I know has been flogged for not reporting, although single junior enlisted service members are typically required to live on base and therefore check in with the Housing Office. However, the Housing Office usually has lists of military-friendly apartment complexes and house rental notices. Better yet, if you want to live in one of these complexes, the Housing Office can usually set you up with a deal to forgo any security deposits, as long as you agree to pay rent by allotment (i.e., directly from your service member's pay and deducted from his paycheck).

The logistical process for obtaining one of these deals or getting on the waiting list is simple: Visit your local base Housing Office. Typically, there is no need for an appointment, although you may want to make one if you need help during peak relocation season. A counselor will be assigned to you and will review your options.

Did You Know?

The military's Sponsorship Program pairs relocating service members with service members already established at the base, usually a future colleague in the new command. The sponsor and his spouse can answer questions and help the relocating family get established in their new community, and overseas sponsors go so far as to help with travel and logistical arrangements. Really great sponsors will even take you out to dinner and introduce you to their friends. Ask your new command or check your service member's orders for information on how to be paired with a sponsor. Knowing how tough it is to relocate, sign up yourself to become a sponsor and help another family with their move.

You can ignore most of this advice if you are relocating overseas. Overseas base Housing Offices are typically much more flexible because they have to be, and they have more housing to accommodate more families. Your relocation counselor can help put you in contact with the Housing Office counselor at your destination base, or see the Military HOMEfront website for contact information.

Finally, if you are researching the base and civilian housing at your destination base, be sure to ask the opinion of women who already live there. By simply posting a question on the discussion forums of CinC House.com, you can often find a gold mine of answers not mentioned in the official relocation propaganda provided to you by your relocation counselor or on Military HOMEfront. This is exactly how you will find out which neighborhoods are termite-infested and which are positively opulent.

Easing the Transition to a New Community

As if moving isn't difficult enough, now you have to help your family settle into a new community. The best thing to do is research in advance as much as possible about local jobs, schools, community activities, and neighborhoods. By doing this research and keeping your family informed of your findings, you will help them adjust their expectations and get excited before you pack your bags.

Getting the kids settled may be the most difficult task. If you're lucky, the kids will start school a month or so after you arrive. This will allow them to get settled in but not be too bored or lonely. If like most families you arrive at the beginning of summer, it is critical to get the kids signed up for as many activities as possible, especially on base. This allows them to meet new friends and realize that they are not the only kids who have gone through this ordeal. An additional benefit of your kids' finding new friends is that you may meet their parents and make new friends yourself!

Understand that when it comes to settling your family in the community, your example will lead the way. Your kids don't know how to get involved in the community, and your service member may be too busy trying to get settled in his job. Yet you know that new friendships and community support are the keys to alleviating your family's transition stress. What can you do? Sign up for community activities such as the PTA and spouse club. Throw a party for your neighbors to get to know them better. Go to your service member's Hail and Farewell command party to get to know his colleagues and their spouses. Above all, don't let exhaustion and stress get to you. Sitting on the couch does not introduce you to new friends.

Preparing yourself and your family for living overseas is a different ball game because of culture shock. Many naive people will tell you to "live like the natives" entirely and forgo anything American. Bullfeathers! That approach only works for one-week vacations, not living semipermanently in a foreign country. While you can learn to appreciate other cultures and get your family excited about seeing the world, you cannot change who you are—and you are Americans! You will discover how unique that is when you arrive at your new destination. So plan to visit local historical sites, eat the food, and learn the language. But don't be embarrassed to fall back on the tightly knit community of American expats when the foreign country becomes too much to take.

Did You Know?

For those who will live in a foreign country where there is no military base nearby, my father has some great advice he learned while stationed in South Korea: When you can't take any more, spend a few hours at the nearest, most American hotel you can find. Even if you can afford only a cup of coffee, it will remind you who you are and reenergize you to face life in a foreign country.

Culture shock is more than just American vs. foreign ways of living. It also can involve severe differences in living standards. If you are moving to a lower-income area, the good news is you can probably afford a fabulous house, maid, and maybe even a nanny! Many a wife who has spent time in Bahrain, for example, has marveled at the palaces and house staff regular military folks acquire upon arrival. Even so, that can protect you only so much from the beggars and squalor often just outside the gates. Again, don't be embarrassed to take a break and fall back on the American expat community. In fact, this is one of the main reasons why the Exchanges operate extensive American-style department stores overseas. Somehow, Tommy Hilfiger fashions and peanut butter make it all feel better. Also, if you or your family are having problems adjusting to your new home, talk to other families about how they deal with culture shock.

Pearls of Wisdom for a Great Move

This chapter attempts to give you all the facts about relocation so you can take control of your destiny. Some things, however, will go out of control. Following are some pearls of wisdom from my girlfriend Dawna and numerous CinCHouse gals who have learned from experience:

❯ Whatever nasty things are said in the six months surrounding a move should not be held against that person and do not reflect on the state of your marriage.

❯ No matter how hard you try, some of your valuables will be lost or damaged during a move. Be grateful that your family members are safe, and take revenge on the movers by pursuing full reimbursement through TMO.

❯ When in doubt about your movers, call the TMO Inspector's Office. Do not allow yourself to argue with your movers or travel people. TMO will send someone immediately to mediate between you and the service providers and ensure that your family is taken care of.

In addition to the week of and moving-out-day checklists on pages 131–33, use this master checklist as you count down to relocation.

Master Relocation Checklist

Weeks to Go	Task
12	Upon receiving orders, your service member should contact TMO and schedule counseling session to submit paperwork.
12	Meet with relocation counselor at FSC and the personnel office to get an estimate of how much DLA and Travel Allowance you will receive. Begin to plot a budget and timeline for travel.
12	If you want to live on base, fax application and a copy of PCS order to the Housing Office to get a control number.
12	Set up a file to track moving and house-hunting expenses. Whatever is not covered by allowances may be tax-deductible.

12	Identify your sponsor at your new command who will answer your questions. Begin researching housing and schools in your new city. If you need child care, search for this now.
12	If you own your home and wish to sell, contact a Realtor to put it on the market immediately. If necessary, negotiate with potential buyers to stay in your home until moving-out day. If you can't sell, get it rented as soon as possible and find a property manager.
11	Make an inventory and take pictures of your household possessions and valuables. Send pictures to homeowners/renters insurance company.
11	Meet with TMO to submit paperwork and provide an estimated weight of your household goods. If you go over your weight allowance, get an estimate from movers to pay for the extra amount and begin saving now.
10	Receive moving dates from TMO. Call movers to schedule a premove meeting. If doing a DITY move, reserve a rental truck.
9	Compile and update your résumé. Determine the best time to quit your current job. If you can, start the job search now.
9	Review family records (legal, medical, insurance, birth certificates) and set aside in a file. Get checkups if needed and obtain copies of your medical records.
9	Check homeowners/renters and automobile insurance to notify of change of address and make sure you are covered in transit.
9	Make sure your bank is located in your new hometown, or sign up with a national bank that caters to the military.

8	Clean out your closets and garage. Hold a yard sale or donate items for the tax deduction.
8	If you want to live off base, hopefully you have narrowed down which neighborhoods you want to live in based on schools, crime, commute, and quality of life. Go house hunting now and try to sign a rental contract.
7	Check school schedules and transfer kids' records.
7	Have fun planning your travel. Turn it into a vacation.
6	Give one month's notice to employer, get a letter of referral, and use the remaining two weeks to plan your move. Begin full-scale job search.
5	Notify your landlord as required by lease. Discuss a time to review your home and get a refund of your security deposit.
5	Drop-dead date for getting off-base housing in your new hometown because current renters will be giving one-month notice.
4	Obtain a change-of-address kit from the post office. Send change-of-address cards to family, friends, and businesses such as your accountant, magazines to which you subscribe, and so forth.
3	While paying your bills, contact utility companies to cut off service and obtain letters of referral. Notify them of forwarding address to receive final bills and refunds of any security deposits. Get a list of utilities in your new hometown from your landlord or real estate agent, and contact them to set up service.
3	Reverify schedule with TMO and movers.

3	Take the pets to the vet and obtain health certifications and medical records.
2	Make reservations for overnight stays during your last night in town and, if appropriate, for your travel.
2	If you are driving, have your car serviced.
2	If you are shipping your car, have it picked up.
1	Notify credit card companies of change of address. You'll need to use the new address when verifying any purchases.
1	Review checklist beginning on page 131 for final week and moving day.

The Least You Need to Know

❯ You will survive relocation no matter where you're planning to move! The military hires professional movers and pays your travel expenses. If you're moving overseas, it will arrange travel for you. Your job is to get advice from TMO, personnel command, and the FSC relocation counselor to watch your budget and learn the rules.

❯ If you get smart about relocation, you can actually make money and have a terrific family vacation!

❯ Base housing is harder to come by than you think. If you wish to live on base, contact the Housing Office as soon as you receive orders. You may have to arrange temporary lodging until your number comes up on the waiting list.

❯ Planning ahead and quickly getting settled in your new community will save you and your family a lot of stress.

RESOURCES

❯ www.cinchouse.com—Visit the Relocation Section for personalized checklists and resources on everything you need to relocate, including finding housing and schools in a safe neighborhood. Don't forget to post a note on the discussion boards to chat with women who already live there and can give you the scoop.

- ❯ perdiem.hqda.pentagon.mil/perdiem/—The Per Diem Committee website allows you to look up your travel pay.
- ❯ Naval Supply Systems Command Household Goods website at www .smartwebmove.navsup.navy.mil can give you estimates for the cost of your move, even if you are in another military branch.
- ❯ pptas.ahf.nmci.navy.mil—FISC Household Goods Audit Team. A Navy site but a great place for any service member to estimate the cost and reimbursement of a DITY move. Sailors also can track their claims.
- ❯ www.ahrn.com—Defense Department base housing website. You can even see pictures and floor plans.
- ❯ greatschools.com—Compare schools with ratings, reviews, and test scores.
- ❯ La Quinta Inns (1-800-531-5900)—The only hotel chain that accepts two well-behaved pets up to 40 pounds at all locations.

CHAPTER 10

Marriage Hoo-ah!

Creating a Family Strategy and Lifetime Dreams

If successful marriages thrive with communication and planning, then unsuccessful marriages are rife with misunderstandings, misguided actions, and resentment. Contrary to most newlyweds' belief, you cannot read each other's mind. If a stranger asked my husband, for example, what he envisioned doing this coming weekend, he'd say we plan to sit on the couch and watch *SportsCenter*. If a stranger asked me, I'd respond that we plan to bathe our kids, go grocery shopping, and have a romantic dinner out. Sometime between now and Friday, we will work out a plan that incorporates elements of both visions of the perfect weekend. But we have to take the time to respectfully ask each other what we want to do and then form a compromise.

If it takes this kind of communication to figure out our weekend plans, it certainly takes even more to figure out our lifetime plans. Not only does each of us have to identify and articulate our dreams and goals for the future, but we also have to compromise with each other and form a strategy to achieve the goals we each have.

Remember: Each person's goals are just as important as the other's. While it may seem easy to allow your service member's career in the military to dictate and drive your life's goals, it is only a recipe for resentment.

151

And why cave in when it is possible to achieve your goals as well as his? To make our family strategy, we use a tool called the Master Plan.

First introduced in the terrific financial planning book *The Savvy Sailor*, by Ralph Nelson, the Master Plan concept starts by plotting your service member's career. Ask these questions:

> › What is your husband's career track? In other words, what does he want to do when he grows up?
> › Which military bases are likely to have positions available for his career track?
> › When is he likely to be promoted?
> › Does he want to stay in the military for his entire career, or should he get out at some point once he's prepped himself for a civilian career? Can he get the military to provide or pay for all of his training?

Armed with this information, you can begin to create a family strategy by charting your service member's proposed career track. Following is an example from *The Savvy Sailor* for a Navy Aviation Technician (AT) named Seaman Besaw.

This career track is right on target. Notice that it takes into account the military's system for relocating and deploying your service member (see chapter 3). It alternates between sea and shore tours for the normal periods of time, and the service member relocates near the same regions.

From this basic career track, and using the information you learned about military finances, you can now begin to plot your service member's future income. Again, we will use the example from *The Savvy Sailor*, which assumes a 2.5 percent pay increase each year.

Notice that this accounting does not include extra pay we already discussed, such as Family Separation Pay or Sea Pay during deployments, but you can treat that as icing on the cake. For now, focus on figuring out how much money your service member will earn. Include pay at 20 years of service, remembering that retirement is calculated as a percentage of pay between the 20- and 30-year marks, depending on which plan you choose. Going back to our Master Plan, we can add information on pay (see chart, page 154).

Year	Age	Career	Rank	Location	Job
2003	20	Boot Camp/A School	E-1-2	Great Lakes, MI	Recruit
2004	21	Sea Tour	E-3	Whidbey Island, WA	Maint. Avion. Br., EAWS
2005	22	Sea Tour	E-4	Whidbey Island, WA	Maint. Avion. Br., EAWS
2006	23	Sea Tour	E-4	Whidbey Island, WA	Maint. Avion. Br., EAWS
2007	24	Sea Tour	E-5	San Diego, CA	Instr. Avion. Sch.
2008	25	Shore Tour	E-5	San Diego, CA	Instr. Avion. Sch.
2009	26	Shore Tour	E-5	San Diego, CA	Instr. Avion. Sch.
2010	27	Shore Tour	E-5	San Diego, CA	Instr. Avion. Sch.
2011	28	Adv. Training	E-6	Jacksonville, FL	Student
2012	29	Sea Tour	E-6	Jacksonville, FL	Workcenter LPO
2013	30	Sea Tour	E-6	Jacksonville, FL	Workcenter LPO
2014	31	Sea Tour	E-6	Jacksonville, FL	Workcenter LPO
2015	32	Sea Tour	E-7	Jacksonville, FL	Workcenter LPO
2016	33	Shore Tour	E-7	Pensacola, FL	Recruiter
2017	34	Shore Tour	E-7	Pensacola, FL	Recruiter
2018	35	Shore Tour	E-7	Pensacola, FL	Recruiter
2019	36	Sea Tour	E-8	Jacksonville, FL	Maint. QA
2020	37	Sea Tour	E-8	Jacksonville, FL	Maint. QA
2021	38	Sea Tour	E-8	Jacksonville, FL	Maint. QA
2022	39	Sea Tour	E-8	Jacksonville, FL	Maint. QA

Adapted from Ralph F. Nelson, *The Savvy Sailor: An Eye-Opening Guide to One Sailor's Personal Financial Saga!* (Rockville, MD: Master Plan, 2002).

Seaman Besaw's Career Pay

Year	Age	Rank	Base Pay	Housing	Food	Clothing	Total
2003	20	E-1-2	$13,820	0 (barracks)	$232	$261	$14,314
2004	21	E-3	$15,642	0	$310	$292	$16,243
2005	22	E-4	$18,668	0	$317	$299	$19,284
2006	23	E-4	$20,167	0	$325	$306	$20,799
2007	24	E-5	$23,629*	0	$333	$314	$24,277
2008	25	E-5	$24,220	$16,186	$3,200	$322	$43,928*
2009	26	E-6	$25,970	$16,591	$3,280	$330	$46,171
2010	27	E-6	$26,619	$17,006	$3,362	$338	$47,325
2011	28	E-6	$32,159	$11,896	$3,446	$347	$47,848
(and so on until you reach 20 years in service. . . .)							
2023	40	E-8	$55,682	$16,788	$4,522	$455	$77,446

*Note the big bump in pay in 2007. While it may seem Seaman Besaw got a pay increase for being promoted to E-5, closer inspection shows that he simply was no longer allowed to live in the barracks and opted for civilian housing. Thus he was given BAH Without Dependents. All of it was put toward rent and utilities.

Adapted from Ralph F. Nelson, *The Savvy Sailor: An Eye-Opening Guide to One Sailor's Personal Financial Saga!* (Rockville, MD: Master Plan, 2002).

Now you can begin to make your own personal, career, and family plans. Ask yourself and then discuss with your service member the following questions:

> ❯ What are your personal and professional goals? Can your career travel with you, or do you need to be stationed in one location?
> ❯ Do you want to try to live in one location as much as possible, or opt for some adventurous travel—or a mix of both?
> ❯ Do you want to have kids, and how do you want to raise them?
> ❯ How can you work the military pay system to earn as much income, retirement, and education benefits as possible?
> ❯ Can your husband hone his career track to fit your family goals?

Let's continue with the example in *The Savvy Sailor*. Seaman Besaw talked extensively with his girlfriend, Susie, and together they decided to get married at age 25, just when the seaman would be leaving his sea tour and starting a shore tour. That way, they could spend the first three years of their marriage uninterrupted by deployment. Susie, however, wanted to continue working, which was fine because San Diego (where they would be stationed) has a very high cost of living. They decided it would be better to wait until the end of his shore tour and the beginning of his advanced training to have a baby. Jacksonville, where training would take place, has a very low cost of living, so they could easily afford to have Susie quit work and stay at home with the baby if she wanted to. Following training, they would try to get a sea tour billet in Jacksonville to maintain family stability with the new baby. They also could have a second child while in Jacksonville. By the end of his sea tour, their first child would be ready to start school, so the Besaws could opt to move close to home by taking a recruiting job in Pensacola. Before they relocate, however, they could afford to buy a home in Jacksonville on Seaman Besaw's salary alone. Then Seaman Besaw could opt for another sea tour billet in Jacksonville and subsequently retire at 20 years if he wished.

Using this strategy, we can add the relevant information to the Besaws' Master Plan (chart, page 157).

The Savvy Sailor is highly recommended to help you develop a more

Year	Age	Career	Rank	Location	Job	Annual Income
2003	20	Boot Camp/A school	E-1-2	Great Lakes, MI	Recruit	$14,314
2004	21	Sea Tour	E-3	Whidbey Island, WA	Maint. Avion. Br., EAWS	16,243
2005	22	Sea Tour	E-4	Whidbey Island, WA	Maint. Avion. Br., EAWS	16,243
2006	23	Sea Tour	E-4	Whidbey Island, WA	Maint. Avion. Br., EAWS	18,668
2007	24	Sea Tour	E-5	San Diego, CA	Instr. Avion. Sch.	18,668
2008	25	Shore Tour	E-5	San Diego, CA	Instr. Avion. Sch.	43,928
2009	26	Shore Tour	E-5	San Diego, CA	Instr. Avion. Sch.	43,928
2010	27	Shore Tour	E-5	San Diego, CA	Instr. Avion. Sch.	43,928
2011	28	Adv. training	E-6	Jacksonville, FL	Student	47,848
2012	29	Sea Tour	E-6	Jacksonville, FL	Workcenter LPO	49,044
2013	30	Sea Tour	E-6	Jacksonville, FL	Workcenter LPO	49,044
2014	31	Sea Tour	E-6	Jacksonville, FL	Workcenter LPO	49,044
2015	32	Sea Tour	E-7	Jacksonville, FL	Workcenter LPO	49,044
2016	33	Shore Tour	E-7	Pensacola, FL	Recruiter	60,573
2017	34	Shore Tour	E-7	Pensacola, FL	Recruiter	60,573
2018	35	Shore Tour	E-7	Pensacola, FL	Recruiter	60,573
2019	36	Sea Tour	E-8	Jacksonville, FL	Maint. QA	70,483
2020	37	Sea Tour	E-8	Jacksonville, FL	Maint. QA	70,483
2021	38	Sea Tour	E-8	Jacksonville, FL	Maint. QA	70,483
2022	39	Sea Tour	E-8	Jacksonville, FL	Maint. QA	77,446

Adapted from Ralph F. Nelson, *The Savvy Sailor: An Eye-Opening Guide to One Sailor's Personal Financial Saga!* (Rockville, MD: Master Plan, 2002).

Year	Age	Career	Rank	Location	Job	Annual Income	Family	Susie's Career	Housing
2003	20	Boot Camp/A school	E-1-2	Great Lakes, MI	Recruit	$14,314		College	Barracks
2004	21	Sea Tour	E-3	Whidbey Island, WA	Maint. Avion. Br., EAWS	16,243		College	Barracks
2005	22	Sea Tour	E-4	Whidbey Island, WA	Maint. Avion. Br., EAWS	16,243		College	Barracks
2006	23	Sea Tour	E-4	Whidbey Island, WA	Maint. Avion. Br., EAWS	18,668		Job	Barracks
2007	24	Sea Tour	E-5	San Diego, CA	Instr. Avion. Sch.	18,668		Job	Barracks
2008	25	Shore Tour	E-5	San Diego, CA	Instr. Avion. Sch.	43,928	Marry/Baby	Job	Rent Apt.
2009	26	Shore Tour	E-5	San Diego, CA	Instr. Avion. Sch.	43,928		Homemaker	Rent Apt.
2010	27	Shore Tour	E-5	San Diego, CA	Instr. Avion. Sch.	43,928		Homemaker	Rent Apt.
2011	28	Adv. training	E-6	Jacksonville, FL	Student	47,848		Homemaker	Rent Buy Home
2012	29	Sea Tour	E-6	Jacksonville, FL	Workcenter LPO	49,044	Baby	Homemaker	Rent Buy Home
2013	30	Sea Tour	E-6	Jacksonville, FL	Workcenter LPO	49,044		Homemaker	Rent Buy Home
2014	31	Sea Tour	E-6	Jacksonville, FL	Workcenter LPO	49,044		Homemaker	Rent Buy Home
2015	32	Sea Tour	E-7	Jacksonville, FL	Workcenter LPO	49,044		Homemaker	Rent Buy Home
2016	33	Shore Tour	E-7	Pensacola, FL	Recruiter	60,573		Continuing Ed.	Rent (Rent Out Home)
2017	34	Shore Tour	E-7	Pensacola, FL	Recruiter	60,573		Continuing Ed.	Rent (Rent Out Home)
2018	35	Shore Tour	E-7	Pensacola, FL	Recruiter	60,573		Continuing Ed.	Rent (Rent Out Home)
2019	36	Sea Tour	E-8	Jacksonville, FL	Maint. QA	70,483		Job	Home
2020	37	Sea Tour	E-8	Jacksonville, FL	Maint. QA	70,483		Job	Home
2021	38	Sea Tour	E-8	Jacksonville, FL	Maint. QA	70,483		Job	Home
2022	39	Sea Tour	E-8	Jacksonville, FL	Maint. QA	77,446		Job	Home

Adapted from Ralph F. Nelson, *The Savvy Sailor: An Eye-Opening Guide to One Sailor's Personal Financial Saga!* (Rockville, MD: Master Plan, 2002).

detailed financial plan for your family, but even using this basic start you can begin to make out your family strategy. *The Savvy Sailor* also includes sample Master Plans for you to fill out. Once you get started, you and your service member will find it exciting! What an opportunity to build your marriage by sharing dreams and goals together.

A Big "If"

Having encouraged you to make a family strategy, I must now give you a very big caveat: You are not guaranteed to get the duty stations you want. You and your service member can make the best of plans, but the military's needs change, and the duty stations you want may not even be open for the taking.

Don't freak out. This is where communication is all the more critical to manage each other's expectations about which dreams are achievable or desirable. By getting into an almost daily habit of discussing dreams and the challenges to those dreams, you and your service member can subtly adjust each other's perceptions about what may be the right path. Then, when something doesn't go right, it's not such a shock and you've already discussed alternatives.

What happens if you desire a certain duty station and it doesn't come up as an option for your service member? The worst-case scenario is that neither you nor your service member did your research on that duty station to find out whether it was open—so the list came as a shock—nor did you discuss alternatives that are acceptable to both of you.

The best-case scenario is that you and your service member did do research on that location and discovered that there aren't many positions available there. There's a chance a post might come up, but it's not very likely. With that in mind, you discuss which duty stations are likely to come up and the pros and cons of each. Part of that discussion is what your family priorities are right now. Do you want to travel to exotic places or stay close to home in a low-cost, family-friendly community? By agreeing in advance and prioritizing your preferences for duty stations, and also prioritizing your goals for the next duty station in general, you won't be surprised when the list arrives. You will already know which duty stations are preferable, even if you didn't expect to see some duty stations on the list.

The importance of getting into the habit of discussing your dreams and challenges also extends to your goals and aspirations. If you are a die-hard career woman and suddenly decide to stay at home with the kids, you will shock the heck out of your service member and probably your family finances as well. If over time, however, you share with him your dissatisfaction with your job, concern about leaving the kids in day care, and ideas for penny-pinching if you were to stay at home, your service member will be on the same mental track with you and the decision won't be so traumatic.

On a final note, don't get angry with your service member if your family strategy has to take a detour because the duty stations you want aren't available. He can't control these things. He can only do his best to research what is available, discuss the options with you, negotiate with his stubborn Job Guy, and hope for the best. It's always tempting to take out your frustration on your service member, but you would be doing him an injustice for all his hard work.

Calling All Military Men: Better Ways to Communicate with Your Wife

Ladies, this section is for your service member to read.

If you have read the previous section on creating a family strategy, you may be freaking out right now. You're thinking, How can this crazy woman suggest to my wife that we have any control over duty stations? The less my wife knows about available duty stations, the less she has to worry about.

This approach is very typical of men who truly just want to make their wives happy. Unfortunately, men and women deal with stress differently. Military men often encourage their wives to "go with the flow" and expect to be sent to Timbuktu. Yet no comment will annoy your wife more, because she wants to *feel* control over her destiny. The family strategy approach suggested herein will allow her to feel in control of the situation, even if you aren't actually in control and don't get the duty stations you want. It's the communication and the compromise that are important. How does this work?

First, understand that by insisting that your wife accept lack of control over the situation, you are indirectly telling her that her dreams don't matter to you or the military. By allowing duty stations to dictate your family's direction, you are saying that your job has priority over her dreams.

By contrast, your wife wants to know you are listening to her dreams and priorities because they count for something in your marriage. And when you listen to her dreams, you are informing yourself about what kind of duty stations are acceptable to her. Then you can come home and say, "You know how you've always wanted to go to Hawaii? Well, I'm not sure the rumor is true, but I heard today that there may be a position opening around the time I'm supposed to get my next orders. Let me find out more information so I can see how likely this would be, but I wanted to let you know." You will get the best sex of your life.

What happens if that Hawaii tour isn't available? Keep her posted on what information you learn so you can manage her expectations. Don't try to shelter her by saying nothing if you hear bad news; share it with her. What's most important about this process is that you are letting her know that you are doing your best to make her dreams come true. If you've done what you can and the duty station doesn't come through, she will know how much you love her and appreciate the effort. In the meantime, you should also be discussing her priorities on duty stations you *know* will be open. When those duty stations show up on the list of options, your wife will be prepared to accept them and confident that you have made the right decision.

Notice how none of this has to do with actually controlling the duty station situation. Instead, this is all about perceived control over the situation because you both have a genuine grasp of what your priorities are as a family. By listening and showing appreciation for your wife's dreams, you are giving her a sense of control. And that makes her happy!

Handling Deployment Separation Together

After the stress of feeling out of control of your life and marriage, deployment and separation are the second hardest things on military marriages. During wartime, deployment lengths have increased to as long as 15 months for soldiers. Other service members, particularly in the Navy and the Air Force, have been plucked from their jobs for a one-year "Individual Augmentation" or IA in a combat zone. The Marines have tended to stick to six-month deployments, but they return for only six months before being deployed again. As noted before, long-term absence typically does not make the heart grow fonder; it makes it more resentful. So you may want to limit the chance and length of deployments to the extent that you can, using your family strategy. There are exceptions to this rule, however, and they can apply to the deployments that will inevitably occur.

Experienced military wives handle deployments more successfully for several reasons. First, they and their service members have created avenues for continuing communication and romance across the distance. The Internet makes it even easier. Regular communication allows the service member to stay involved in the family's daily life and remain a principal parent and decision maker. By keeping the service member informed about the family's daily activities, you don't have to write a book to explain and ask advice on the inevitable crises that will pop up during his absence. He will already be up to date on what's brewing and can quickly respond with his thoughts.

It's important that this regular sharing of information not be a one-way stream of complaints from you. Be assured that your service member misses you heartily, and he is worried about leaving you on your own no matter how competent you are. Most of all, he feels guilty. To top it off, he is probably working like a dog and clocking 18-hour days doing dangerous tasks. When you send him nothing but complaints, you worsen his negative feelings and may even distract him from his job. Not only does this ultimately hurt your marriage, it also may make him dangerous to himself and his colleagues. There is nothing your service member can do to make you feel better about deployment and handling life on your own.

Service Members: What to Say to Your Wife

Never say . . .	Instead, say this . . .
Go with the flow.	These are the duty stations that are likely to be available, given my career track. Which ones are you interested in?
We'll never be able to get a post at . . .	To get a post at . . . , it will mean I have to do X, Y, and Z, and we will probably have to live at A. That seems like quite a challenge for our family. Are you sure you want to do that?
I don't know what duty station will be available. No one ever does! I don't care what your friends say.	It's hard to say at this point, but given my career track, I'm likely to get duty stations at A, B, and C. Which of those interest you? or Let's go through the possible scenarios.
I refuse to live there!	I really do not want to take that job. The job is really bad and would require me to do X, Y, and Z. I could see my unhappiness would really make the family miserable. Isn't there another duty station you might find acceptable?
I know you heard there might be a position open at X, but there's no way we'll get it.	Interesting news! However, I have heard that that position requires someone with more qualifications than I have. Why don't I do some more research and see what I can find out?

He cannot leave his station, and he cannot come to your rescue. So please think before you write.

Successful military families are also talented digital photographers and web masters. To share their daily lives together, they regularly take pictures and videos to exchange by e-mail or place on a family website. It is just as important for the service member to take pictures as it is for the kids. How else can you understand what his job entails or get to know his colleagues and friends? (Note: Obviously, any service member in special operations is exempt from this because his job is classified. So don't get mad at him!)

With this daily information sharing, leaving for deployment and returning home become much easier transitions. Your service member will already be aware of and support any new rules you have imposed on your children, and he will feel less guilty about having left his family. He won't feel the need to spoil the kids with ice cream every night or let them bend every rule. You and the kids, in turn, will not view him as a total stranger when he returns, nor resent him when he tries to reassert his authority as a parent and reassume his role as a spouse.

Along with the sharing of daily family news, successful military couples keep up the intensity of their romance through regular communication. While X-rated e-mails are inappropriate because all e-mail into the unit may be read for security purposes, you can develop a more subtle approach using coded words that only he knows. Also, don't send pornographic pictures of yourself, or you may find them plastered all over the Internet. Instead, send him regular care packages with his favorite foods, phone cards, and less risqué pictures of you and the kids.

On the other side of the relationship, he should call you whenever possible, even if it is for only a few minutes. If he can talk for only a short time, assure him how grateful you are just to hear his voice. He will find a way to call you back, even if it means waiting in the phone line for hours! Along the same lines, be sure to let him know how much you enjoy hearing about his day and receiving pictures. He'll appreciate your interest in his life and feel that you understand the stress he is under.

If regular communication is the primary force behind successful military marriages, a sense of independence and self-esteem on your part is the other element.

Struggling wives spend too much time wallowing in their own depression. They honestly believe that the sole source of their happiness is their service member—as if they'd never been happy in their entire lives before they met him! They spend a lot of time moping on the couch.

Did You Know?

Experienced military wives sometimes look forward to deployment. They see it as an opportunity to do the things they wouldn't otherwise have time to do, such as continuing their education, taking a karate or ballet class, or moving back home to spend more time with friends and family members.

If you are one of these wives, my advice is to get up and get busy. Surely there are tons of things you've always wanted to do but never had the opportunity—so do them! While you're at it, meet friends for dinner. And volunteer to help people less fortunate than you are—and there are plenty. They will be your reminder of how lucky you are to be you.

One of the best ways to keep busy is to get involved with your command family support unit to prepare an elaborate homecoming party. This amazing event is often on the minds of families and service members everywhere, and your service member and his colleagues will gossip like hens about what the families have planned. The possibilities are endless and get more elaborate every year. My personal favorite is the 400-foot-plus Hawaiian leis that Navy families string around the ship when it arrives in port. This is your chance to show off your creativity and let your service member know how much you're looking forward to his return.

Finally, while your service member is deployed, you will need the resources to take care of yourself and your family. Plan ahead before deployment to make sure these resources are available. For example, mothers of young children should plan for a babysitter once per week so you can get out of the house and away from the kids. Whether you pay for a babysitter or have your mom babysit, make the arrangements in advance so you don't get stuck. Similarly, working moms need to find logistical support services and the money to pay for them. Whether it's day care, emergency babysitters, lawn mowing, or grocery delivery, you will need help in replacing the extra hands your service member provided when he was home.

However, you also *will* face crises during deployments. I call it the Murphy's Law of the Military: The moment my husband deploys, the car will break down, the plumbing will burst, and the roof will leak. Actually, my personal plague has to do with rodents setting up shop once my pest control guy has carried his seabag out the door. The bottom line is that I have to know how to address these crises or have the financial sources available. I have to be able to fix a car tire, navigate Home Depot for plumber's putty, and have enough savings for a transmission repair (or two). By planning ahead, you can prevent and defuse the inevitable crises that will pop up during deployments. When you remain unprepared, you make your service member worry about you—and that distracts him and creates a danger to himself and his colleagues.

Extra Parenting Skills for Military Couples

Military parents need extra skills to help their kids cope with military life. Military kids move frequently and have to make friends quickly and start at new schools. My own mother, a Navy brat, moved 14 times in 16 years.

Military kids also face the loneliness of separation from their parent during deployments and, worse, may worry about their parent's safety. Indeed, too much CNN for kids is not a good thing!

I've talked about the importance of getting your family settled into a new community as quickly after relocation as possible. Start with setting up your kids' rooms to look as much like their old rooms as possible. Choose decorations, including wall art, that can travel with you.

Before you relocate, identify fun activities in your new hometown and sign your kids up. With any luck, by the second week of moving in, your kids will already be distracted from the stress of moving and focused on having fun with new friends. If you can manage it, invite your new neighbors over for a barbeque so your kids can meet other kids on the block.

Above all, encourage your kids to be as social as possible. This is tougher for shy kids but is an important skill to succeed. You can help them by practicing how to introduce themselves to friends, engage in conversation, and share toys.

Deployments are more difficult because you face emotional issues similar to those in divorce. Your kids may feel like the parent is leaving them because of something they did, so be straightforward with your children that deployment is just part of Daddy's or Mommy's job and that he or she is coming back as soon as the job is done. Immediately after breaking the news of deployment, begin discussing ways to keep in touch, to reassure your kids that the parent is still part of the family.

Did You Know?

When discussing issues of discipline with your kids, be sure to mention that your service member was included in the decision making. For example, you can tell your little girl that Mommy and Daddy agreed that she is too young right now to get her ears pierced, but that Daddy said he would take her to get it done when he got back from deployment. This prevents you from being the "bad guy" all the time.

For example, buy an inexpensive camera for your kids to take pictures with and send to the deployed parent. They can even take the camera to school and snap photos of friends. Older kids can get started on developing a family website on which to place pictures and videos. Another good idea is to get the kids involved in planning homecoming activities as soon as the service member leaves. Maybe homecoming is a good time to plan a family vacation at Disneyland? If so, the service member can put in for leave now.

Finally, let the kids know that just because Daddy is gone doesn't mean he's not still in charge as a parent. Similarly, if a stepparent is being left in charge of the kids, the service member must insist that her word goes while he's gone. The kids should understand that the parents are keeping in touch and will continue to administer discipline as a team. By keeping Daddy involved, you will feel like you still have a backup parent, and the kids will respect his authority when he comes home. Daddy also will feel relieved that he is still valued as a parent.

When Daddy is involved in war or combat, the stress of deployment goes to a higher level. Again, you need to be straightforward with your kids that Daddy is at war, but reassure them how strong and courageous he is and that he and his troops will prevail. It helps to discuss combat in terms of "fighting the bad guys" because it makes kids proud of what their parent is doing and justifies the sacrifice of separation. Young children also are reassured by the idea that a guardian angel is watching over Daddy and "the good guys."

If you absolutely need to watch CNN, do it on your own time and limit your kids' exposure. They don't need their worries about Daddy increased and imprinted on their little brains. Also, watch television with your kids and make sure they know the difference between violence on TV and real violence. It sometimes helps if Daddy explains what it is really like on the battlefield (deleting any explicit references to gory details, of course) compared to what is shown on TV.

During deployments, it's important to keep teachers and other adults notified so that they can warn you of any trouble and work with you to counsel your kids on dealing with the stress. Schools near military bases frequently have specialized counselors for this exact reason, so don't be afraid to use their knowledge if you need help. Finally, remember that your kids need a break from you, too. Schedule time for them with friends or favorite babysitters so they can do fun things and not worry about their family.

In the end, it is impossible to address every crisis and emotional trend you will encounter with deployments, which is why there is a thriving resource at CinCHouse.com. Literally hundreds of thousands of visitors go to CinCHouse.com each month to get answers and just plain vent. And that is another tool in your toolbox.

The Least You Need to Know

> A solid military marriage requires planning your life together and constantly communicating your dreams and ways to overcome obstacles.

> While you cannot guarantee that you'll get the duty stations you want, you can limit the chance of getting a particularly nasty duty station by researching and planning ahead.

> Deployment is stressful on marriage, but you can get through it by maintaining regular communication and keeping busy with friends and fun activities. Experienced wives actually look forward to deployments!

> Military parents need to help their kids learn social skills and get settled into new communities quickly. They must also ease the stress of deployments on kids through honest communication, regular contact, and maintaining two-parent discipline. Combat deployments require extra sensitivity to kids' worries about the safety of their parent.

CHAPTER 11

The Adventures *of* Military Life

Military life can be very exciting, and not just because you can get a military discount at most stores (be sure to ask!). There are tips and tricks for making things fun and easy, and this chapter reviews just a few of them:

1. Furnishing a military household with worldwide treasures
2. How to vacation at almost no cost
3. Children's activities and hobbies (for kids ages two to 92)

Furnishing a Military Household

Whether you're a bride-to-be or a seasoned military wife, it is always a good idea to consider the military lifestyle when buying furniture or household items. Similarly, as you purchase souvenirs from your travels, you want to make sure you're investing in something that will stand the test of time and home decor. After all, these can be high-priced items that will hopefully last a lifetime or longer. There are two things to consider when stocking up your household inventory: frequent moving and the need for storage.

The typical military family moves every three years. That means having burly guys pack up your good china and collectibles. So consider the following tips:

> When entering military life, it's probably not a good idea to start collecting antique teacups or glass figurines.
> If you insist on having good china, select durable china patterns such as Wedgwood with colors that are baked in instead of painted on. Patterns with gold rims may look durable, but it is really gold paint that chips off in the dishwasher.
> Choose thick crystal or glassware instead of the delicate, thin kind.
> Let professional movers pack your china and breakables, but tell them how delicate they are. They'll do a better job than you will, and you can be fully reimbursed for anything broken.

Military families also tend to live in base housing or rentals—and that means a lot of white walls, kitchens, and bathrooms. Despite your best decorating intentions, you are not likely to paint, so you're better off strategizing with a solid decorating theme that will look good whether you're stationed in Japan or California or Washington, D.C.

> When buying your first pieces of furniture, select a general color scheme for the entire house. Every time you buy a new piece, make sure it fits into that scheme—even if it is for a different room. In a few years, all of your furniture may end up in the same room, so it has to coordinate.

> Do not select color schemes with neutral colors such as white, beige, or black. Your walls in base housing or rental homes will always be white or beige, so you'll need to brighten things up with color.

> Buy wooden picture frames and shelves that can be painted. It's a great way to spiff up the inevitable white walls of your base housing or rental.

› Recognize that "California Casual"–style furniture does not look good everywhere. When selecting the cloth for your furniture, choose patterns that will fit in wherever you go. Then use inexpensive tablecloths, curtains, and decorative pillows to make your look more casual or more formal.

› Good-quality used wood, antique, or foreign-made furniture are great collectibles; they're inexpensive, and they capture the memories of where you once lived. In Washington, D.C., for example, you can get a beautiful dark-wood clothes drawer (circa 1900) at local antiques fairs for about $70. Japanese "stair" chests are another great investment.

› When you've finally convinced your husband that the Budweiser Girls are not considered art, contemplate buying a mirror instead of a large poster or painting. They're less expensive than good art, and they brighten a room and go with all decor.

Finally, the biggest challenge for military families is switching from single-family homes in low-cost areas to apartments or town homes in high-cost areas. How do you fit an entire house full of furniture into an apartment without giving half of it away? Following are some tips to address all these problems:

› Invest in a good sofa bed. They're more expensive than regular sofas, but you can put them in the living room or in a guest room.

› Use laminated bookshelves that must be assembled but can be taken apart for easy storage. Buy one neutral color (such as black or white) so they can be mixed and matched in any room. They can be used for books, children's rooms, clothes storage in closets, and garages, or dismantled and packed away in minimal space.

› For storing china, consider buying corner cabinets instead of traditional rectangular monstrosities that take up an entire wall. Triangular in shape, corner cabinets hold a lot more than you think and can fit in almost any room. They're harder to find, but usually you can buy them in any style at your favorite furniture store.

> When choosing bedside tables or end tables, select ones with drawers for extra storage space.

> Get a library card. Buying books costs more money than you think, and their accumulated weight takes up too much of your allocated shipping weight. They also require a lot of storage.

> Avoid buying tchotchkes, trinkets, or bric-a-brac—especially delicate items—at any cost. If you want to collect memories, get your family interested in photography. Inexpensive jewelry is another option that collects less dust and requires less space.

> Every three months, make your entire family review their clothes and belongings, and give away any item that has not been used in the past year. Not only will this improve storage and packing time, it also will force every family member to think twice before buying something.

If you do have to give away furniture and sundries, make an effort to give them to another military family. We all reap the benefits in the end.

How to Vacation at Almost No Cost

Did you know that you can fly to Europe for a family vacation at the military's expense? Space Available or "Space A" flights are one of the great benefits of military life. Essentially, the military has regular transport planes of all types flying around the world. Not only do they move equipment, they also transport relocating families and officials on business. Often there is plenty of extra space available on overseas flights to take on passengers, so the military allows service members and their dependents to fly Space Available. The military also allows family members of deployed service members to fly Space A within CONUS.

The trick is that while the flights run on a regular schedule, there is no guarantee that a seat will be available for you. You may have to wait for the next flight or the flight after that before boarding a jet to Italy.

The pros say the downsides are still worth the ability to travel globally. Desiring romantic time together before a six-month deployment, my girlfriend Belle and her Marine husband spent two weeks in Italy over Easter. When their return flight wasn't immediately available in Italy, they used the excuse to spend a couple of days in Germany and fly home from there. To save money, the couple stayed at base lodging and packed lunches from the commissaries. It was the experience of a lifetime—at a grand total cost of $500 for the whole trip!

Base lodging is another great deal. Nearly all military bases worldwide offer the ability to stay at a base "lodge" or hotel or the Bachelor Enlisted/ Officers' Quarters (**BEQ** or **BOQ**). Some of these are so popular they get booked a year in advance. Our favorite places include the BOQ and Navy Lodge at NAS North Island, on the white beaches of San Diego, and the Navy Lodge at NAS Key West, where you can rent a motorboat for a few dollars per day. More famous destinations are the Hale Koa military hotel on Waikiki Beach in Hawaii and the Shades of Green resort for military families at Disney World in Orlando, Florida.

While there are a number of lodging and Transportation Command websites (www.spacea.info) with Space A schedules and regulations, I recommend investing in copies of *Military Space-A: Air and Temporary Military Lodging Around the World,* published by Military Living Publications. These and other terrific guides, such as *Military RV: Camping & Outdoor Recreation Around the World,* can be found at your base Exchange, or online at www.militaryliving.com.

Children's Activities (for Kids from Two to 92)

Because so many military families have young children, the Morale, Welfare, and Recreation (**MWR**) offices and Marine Corps Community Services (**MCCS**) offer tons of activities for families with children.

One of my regular stops is the Information, Tickets, & Tours (**ITT**) office for free or significantly discounted tickets to rock concerts, theaters, movies, kids' events, and major theme parks, including Disneyland and Busch Gardens. ITT also frequently puts together travel packages for groups of families to visit more distant locations, particularly theme parks. It's worth a quick stop to receive a flyer with all available discounts listed.

MWR and MCCS also offer summer day camps and after-school activities ranging from sports to arts and crafts. Adults can get in on the fun at the numerous woodworking shops, pottery classes, and other activities offered by MWR and MCCS. My favorite class so far has been Kahuna Bob's Surfing Lessons at Camp Pendleton, California.

For those who want to get outside, MWR and MCCS rent outdoor and party equipment for pennies. This equipment is typically tailored to your local area, so you will find horse trailers and stables in rural areas, and beach tents and chairs near the coastlines. Folding chairs and tables and other equipment also are available for parties.

The USO also frequently holds large events such as concerts, kids' days at the zoo, and holiday parties. These are typically free or steeply discounted, so keep an eye on their local website or the base newspaper.

Finally, every military base offers plenty of recreation and athletic facilities. The Air Force is famous for its golf courses and the Navy for its beaches. Most bases also have several pool facilities, including many at the center of base housing complexes, and the best gymnasiums, with top-of-the-line equipment and the latest aerobics classes. Most bases operate team sports leagues and competitions for both adults and children, so visit your nearest gym for brochures on upcoming events and activities.

The Least You Need to Know

> When buying household furniture, be aware that items have to fit with the decor of your entire household in any location around the world.
> Collecting furniture and photos from the places where you live is a great way to save memories while minimizing clutter.
> The freebies you get in the military mean you can plan a virtually cost-free vacation.

> MWR, MCCS, and the USO are your sources for unique and fun activities for you and the kids. Check their offices and the base newspaper regularly for the latest events and offers.

RESOURCES

> Space A Flights (www.spacea.info)—Find free flights anywhere in the world.
> Military Living Publications (www.militaryliving.com)—Terrific books on cheap travel deals through the military.
> The Navy Lodge (www.navy-lodge.com).
> www.armymwr.com, www.mwr.navy.mil, www.afsv.af.mil, and www.usmc-mccs.org—The national websites for MWR and MCCS, but be sure to check your base website for local MWR or MCCS sites promoting activities and resources in your area.
> Marine Corps Community Services (www.usmc-mccs.org).
> Air Force Crossroads (www.afcrossroads.com)—This section has tons of travel and recreation activities.
> Check your base website for local MWR or MCCS activities.

More ideas, from Lindsey of Sheppard AFB, Texas:

Use liquid fabric starch to adhere fabric to walls. Small pieces of cutout fabric can be used as "stencils," and larger pieces of fabric (including flat bedsheets) work as "wallpaper."

Simply immerse your desired fabric, already cut to shape, in a bucket of liquid fabric starch (available at most commissaries for less than $2 a bottle). Wring out any excess. Using a sponge dampened with water, smooth the fabric onto the wall, pressing out any air bubbles. Wipe any drips with a damp sponge or cloth. Allow the fabric to dry. When it is time to move, fill a spritzer bottle with water and gently moisten the fabric on the walls. The fabric will easily peel away, leaving the walls clean and white again!

While in Europe, I made simple curtains for my child's bedroom. Using cut patches of the extra fabric, I created a stencil effect on the walls. When it was time to PCS, I packed the curtains and the stencil patches into a bag and took them to the thrift shop, along with the "how to" directions. They sold right away, and now another child's room has been decorated with very little effort!

Note: Removable wallpaper "stickies" found at Wal-Mart and Home Depot also have the same effect. Buy an extra set to take to your next duty station in case the old ones don't restick.

CHAPTER 12

What Happens When *the* Worst Happens— *and* What *to* Do

No one expects the worst to happen, so we tend not to plan in advance. Fortunately, the military does, and there are resources in place to support you and your family in times of need.

When You Must Live Near an Ailing Family Member

If you must temporarily live near your immediate family, such as your parents or children living with an ex-spouse, service members can be considered for a Humanitarian Transfer to a duty station nearby. They may have to delay their career progress, they may not enjoy their position, and they may not even be stationed on a base in their service. The main point, however, is not to deny a service member his or her right to help a family member in extreme need.

If You Must Separate from an Abusive Spouse

The 1995 DoD Authorization Act requires the Armed Forces to provide monthly payments to spouses and eligible children of active duty service members who are separated from the military due to family abuse. This compensation may be awarded for a period of one to three years. The purpose is to prevent financial hardship on spouses who report abuse and whose service members are incarcerated as a result. Contact the Family Advocacy representative in your base family support center for more information.

When Your Service Member's Pay Gets Screwed Up and You Have No Money for Groceries or Bills

Pay problems happen all the time because of administrative errors as well as mismanagement due to the complicated nature of our benefits. For example, when a service member goes on an extended deployment, his pay is docked for BAS, since he will now be eating with his unit. That's big bucks to a wife who had counted on that money to make ends meet. The Navy–Marine Corps Relief Society, Army Emergency Relief, Air Force Aid Society, and American Red Cross were set up to help families with financial planning and provide interest-free loans and grants for temporary financial problems.

When You Have Emergency Expenses

Whether the car suddenly breaks down or you need money to visit your dying parent, the Navy–Marine Corps Relief Society, Army Emergency Relief, Air Force Aid Society, and American Red Cross can provide interest-free loans and grants for qualifying emergencies.

When You Desperately Need to Track Down a Deployed Service Member

The American Red Cross can send emergency messages to deployed service members—but only if they are genuine emergencies. It is critical that you know your service member's Social Security number, rank, unit, and location (such as a base, camp, or ship). Don't be a nitwit by not knowing these obviously important details! Call your base operator for the number to the American Red Cross on base. Red Cross offices located off base may not be aware of this service provided to military family members.

When Both Parents or a Single Parent Is in the Military and Forced to Deploy

The military tries to work with dual-service member families to ensure that the kids are cared for. Otherwise, it risks losing both service members because of the difficulty of parenting. Unfortunately, if both parents or a single service member is called to deploy, the parent has no choice but to deploy. There are extremely rare exceptions, but don't count on being one. By being excused from deployment, the service member's duties are an extra burden on the shoulders of his or her colleagues.

Additionally, the military does not provide for the cost of child care during deployments. Your only choice is to anticipate deployments and plan ahead with family and friends to care for your child. Dual-service member parents and single-service member parents are required to submit forms known as a Family Care Plan. This plan not only shows that you have thought through who will take care of your children but also that you have obtained the caregiver's consent and have filled out all of the necessary legal and financial documents that will put the plan into effect should you deploy. Failure to maintain a current Family Care Plan on file with your unit is grounds for separation from the service.

When a Service Member Dies

When an active-duty service member dies, a command representative and the Decedent Affairs Officer (in the Army, the Notification Officer) come to inform the family. The Decedent Affairs Officer helps make funeral arrangements and "invitational travel orders" for immediate family members to attend the funeral.

Then the Casualty Assistance Calls Officers (**CACO**s)—in the Army, the Casualty Assistance or Mortuary Affairs Officers—help survivors apply for the benefits entitled to them. Sometimes the CACO comes with a $100,000 check in hand for the death gratuity, the purpose of which is primarily to cover funeral and other expenses. The surviving dependents also are entitled to Dependents Indemnity Compensation from the Veterans Administration and Service Members' Group Life Insurance (SGLI—yes, that $26 per month may come in handy one day). Finally, a surviving spouse is entitled to receive Survivor Benefit Compensation as part of the service member's retired pay, if the service member died while still on active duty but was otherwise eligible to retire.

When Your Man Comes Home "Changed"

The good news in today's military is that the risk of your service member getting killed in combat is very low. Protective gear, strategic maneuvers, and excellent medical treatment have all helped protect our service members. However, there is a higher chance that your service member will return from deployment with mental or physical changes—some subtle and others requiring a lifetime of care.

First I will address the more widespread but subtle issues of post-traumatic stress disorder (PTSD) and traumatic brain injuries (**TBI**). It's telling that the standard operating assumption in the Army is that approximately 20 to 30 percent of soldiers in combat will return home with PTSD or a TBI or both.

According to the National Institute of Mental Health, PTSD is an anxiety disorder that can develop after exposure to a terrifying event or ordeal in which grave physical harm occurred or was threatened.

Traumatic events that may trigger PTSD include violent personal assaults, natural or human-caused disasters, accidents, or military combat. Military wives sometimes see the results of PTSD when their service members come home and can't sleep, or react violently when children make a loud noise, and begin abusive behavior. Don't kid yourself: In severe form, PTSD can make a service member suicidal or homicidal, and it must be treated immediately. In less severe cases, service members need time to adjust to American society, and you need to be sensitive. There are many anecdotal situations of husbands freaking out while driving under a bridge (bridges are a common source of Improvised Explosive Devices [**IEDs**] in Iraq) or becoming overwhelmed by the noise in a Wal-Mart. You need to monitor that situation and act accordingly.

Because PTSD is purely a mental health issue, it has had a terrible stigma in the past, and many service members refuse treatment for fear it will go on their service record. Yet in just the past two years, things have changed drastically because the military establishment has realized that even the best and bravest are afflicted. So, for example, a service member will no longer lose his security clearance because he receives mental health care for PTSD. And with almost a third of all deployed soldiers, your service member is in good company—so make him get help if he becomes depressed or uncontrollable. Also, talk to his buddies in the unit to find out what happened, and work with them to help your man talk things through. Wives and command buddies are the first line of protection.

A TBI is a trauma to the head that disrupts brain function and can range between mild (a brief, reversible change in mental status) to severe (an extended period of dysfunction or amnesia). So, for example, if your service member is knocked off his feet by an IED, even if he suffered no other wounds, it is likely that the shock wave may have rolled through his brain and caused some problems. What causes TBI?

> Bullets, fragments, blasts
> Falls
> Motor vehicle-traffic crashes
> Assaults

The sooner he and you recognize the symptoms, the sooner he'll get treatment and the more likely he is to recover. These symptoms include:

> Dizziness
> Excessive fatigue (tiredness)
> Concentration problems
> Forgetting things
> Irritability
> Sleep problems
> Balance problems
> Ringing in the ears
> Vision changes not improving

Source: Deployment Health Clinical Center.

Because this is a physical injury, the symptoms tend to be more physical, and there is less stigma associated with treatment. Resources for families are improving and, according to a Defense Department announcement, the Defense Centers of Excellence for Psychological Health and Traumatic Brain Injury (**DCoE**) has opened a 24-hour outreach center to provide information and referrals to military service members, veterans, their families, and others with questions about psychological health and traumatic brain injury. The new center can be contacted around the clock, 365 days a year, by phone at 1-866-966-1020 and by e-mail at resources@dcoeoutreach.org.

What Happens When Your Service Member Is Seriously Wounded

If your service member is "hit," the first things you need to be assured of is:

> The military is extraordinarily good at medical care of wounded service members, and there is an excellent chance of his surviving and thriving even in the worst-case scenarios.
> They will call and notify you because they understand the need to have you by his bedside as soon as possible.

The first step will come in a phone call from the deployed unit. If your service member is conscious, and many are, he will call you directly in the hope of hearing your voice. Either way, they will tell you what happened, give their honest assessment of his situation, and tell you what the next step is.

That next step for the service member is probably a quick flight to Landstuhl Hospital in Germany, followed by a subsequent flight to a major MTF in the United States that focuses on wounded care. Thus your next call will be from the hospital staff at Landstuhl, updating you on his situation. If the situation is serious, they may not be able to move him and will likely send you Invitational Orders (the first flight out) to be by his side. That's not likely, however, since most wounded are stabilized and the service member promptly sent on, typically to Walter Reed Army Medical Center or National Naval Medical Center (Bethesda) near Washington, D.C., or Brooke Army Medical Center (**BAMC**) in San Antonio, Texas. No matter what service he is in, he will likely be sent to one of these three hospitals, and you will receive Invitational Orders from the hospital command to join him as soon as possible. The folks issuing your orders are pretty darn quick about racing you out there, so fight the urge to buy the next (and most expensive) flight out. You will need that money very soon. Instead, pack a suitcase, notify your job, and arrange for people to take care of your kids, your pets, and anything else that needs attention. Your sole job now is to help him get better.

Your Invitational Orders should provide you with transportation to and accommodations near the hospital. Someone will pick you up from the airport, and you will probably stay a week or two, depending on the situation. Keep a manila envelope with you and shove any and all receipts in it. You will need reimbursement later.

This is where your money will start to run out. It's the last thing you will want to think of, but paying attention to your finances will be critical to your long-term success as a couple. Take five minutes away from his bedside and meet all the caseworkers and fellow wounded caregivers you can. Army Wounded Warrior (**AW2**), the Soldier and Family Assistance Center (**SFAC**), the DFAS Wounded Warrior Pay Team, and all the nonprofit staff are there to provide solutions. You need another plane ticket to check on things at home and come back to his bedside? There are programs for that. You need Grandma to stay with the kids while you're gone? There are programs for that. You lost your job after so much time away, and you need financial support to pay the mortgage? There are programs for that. Why? *Because these are the kinds of things that regularly happen with wounded warrior families.* They have enough problems without having to worry about financial difficulties. The massive breadth of options and opportunities can be found at the National Resource Directory at www.nationalresourcedirectory.org.

Navigating your service member's pay and entitlements is important for this reason. Although the regulations continue to change and improve for wounded warriors, the first thing you should check is that he is continuing to receive pay as if he were still deployed to a combat zone, specifically Hardship Duty Pay, Hostile Fire Pay, Family Separation Pay, BAS, and Combat Zone Tax Exclusion. The DFAS Wounded Warrior Pay Team can personally assist you in identifying any glitches and filling out armloads of forms, including for your travel. You can also find their website at www.dfas.mil/militarypay/woundedwarriorpay.html.

Once your service member has completed any emergency care, you will likely be moved to nearby temporary housing such as Fisher House or Mologne House. The good news is that the military will pay for the entire family to relocate, so no more expensive flights home. The bad news is that you will have to fit the entire family into these hotel-style rooms and share a communal kitchen with other families. That can be helpful in finding friends who have the same problems, but living in such close quarters is inevitably stressful. One family I know regularly put their baby to bed in the bathtub so he would sleep without the family waking him. So much for midnight trips to go pee. If you have a larger family, some nonprofit organizations will provide housing, just ask your caseworker who the reputable ones are.

Once your service member is out of the hospital, or close to it, your caseworker will urge you to apply for TSGLI, an entitlement for severe losses (such as a lost arm or leg). TSGLI coverage will pay a benefit from $25,000 to $100,000 depending on eligibility and the severity of the loss resulting from traumatic injury. For more information contact the Office of SGLI by phone at 1-800-419-1473, or visit the TSGLI website at:

www.insurance.va.gov/sgliSite/TSGLI/TSGLI.htm. As a guardian or with a power of attorney, you may fill out this paperwork for him. This is important because you may have some debt to pay off, and once he leaves the hospital he will start to lose some of his combat pay and entitlements.

By now your husband is completing any additional surgeries and beginning therapy. If he's basically back to normal, he may be sent back to his previous unit, where he returns to duty. Otherwise, he may be placed in a Wounded Transition Unit. At this point you will begin the Disability Retirement Process to determine whether the service member should be separated from service (i.e., forced to leave) or medically retired (with pay for life) or otherwise receive some kind of entitlement pay for life.

Again, the process for disability assessment is evolving because of all the complaints in the past, but your service member will essentially go through two disability boards: one from his branch of service (Physical Evaluation Board or **PEB**), and the other from the Department of Veterans' Affairs (**VA**). Through the process, you should work very closely with nonprofit staff and military caseworkers to finish the paperwork and present the best case possible. They will make themselves available to you at the hospitals and other common areas for wounded families, or look for sources on the National Resource Directory at www.national resourcedirectory.org. A lifetime of services and pay depends on his disability rating. A disability rating of 30 percent is the magic number. If your service member is rated at less than 30 percent, he will be separated from the military with no pay. That poses a problem for those with ongoing medical needs, and you run the risk of never being able to obtain life or health insurance. If he already has 20 years in the service, they will retire him with retirement pay and lifetime medical benefits.

If you get 30 percent, then at least he gets health care for life and all other privileges of a military retiree. This includes disability retirement pay for life according to the larger option: Method A is based on the disability percentage, while Method B is based on the years of active service. He also may apply for a variety of other lifetime payments: disability compensation from the VA, Social Security disability, and possibly Combat-Related Special Compensation or Concurrent Retirement and Disability Pay.

The Survivor Benefit Plan is also paid to you, the spouse, as 55 percent of his retirement pay when he dies, unless you remarry. If the retiree dies of service-related illness, as certified by a physician, or if a 100 percent veteran dies after 10 years of eligibility, you may also be entitled to Dependency and Indemnity Compensation.

At this stage, the payments get extra-complicated. My recommendation is to get some more detailed books on the subject. Additionally, you'll need to work with professionals to address your individual situation and protect your family's interests.

The Least You Need to Know

> Monitor your service member for signs of PTSD and TBI when he returns from a deployment, and if necessary get help immediately.
> If your service member is wounded, you will be quickly notified and provided assistance to get you by his bedside as quickly as possible.
> The process of being wounded can bankrupt your family, so protect yourself by hooking up with good resources.
> Work closely with caseworkers and nonprofit organizations when navigating your pay and disability process. Your family's future may be greatly impacted by the decisions you make now.

ADDITIONAL RESOURCES

> Outreach Center for Psychological Health and Traumatic Brain Injury— Call 1-866-966-1020 or e-mail resources@dcoeoutreach.org.
> www.nationalresourcedirectory.org—National Resource Directory.
> www.dfas.mil/militarypay/woundedwarriorpay.html—DFAS Section pay and entitlements for wounded warriors.
> www.insurance.va.gov/sgliSite/TSGLI/TSGLI.htm—Department of Veterans' Affairs section on TSGLI, but there tons of other great information on pay and entitlement.

CHAPTER 13

Preventing Trouble *in* Paradise

Having seen so many women succeed in or struggle with military life, I've found that there are generally eight predictors of success:

1. *Embracing the benefits and keeping a positive outlook*—Mental attitude and the ability to adapt to change are the major predictors of success or struggle with military life. If you can look for opportunity in every change of circumstance, you will have the experience of a lifetime and amazing stories to tell your friends back home. For example, if you are assigned to a duty station in London, England, would you rather remember the experience as dining with the Queen or being forced to live thousands of miles away from your home country and not meeting any new friends? It's the same location, but the experience is up to you. Personally, I'd rather dine with the Queen.

2. *Learning about military life and what to expect*—Some women express their resentment at the perceived lack of control over their lives by refusing to learn about military life. Yet if your service member

held a civilian job, would you refuse to let him talk about it at home or meet his colleagues? Not only is this attitude harmful to your marriage, it also hampers your ability to get the information needed to control your family's destiny. If you resent military life, express it in a less self-destructive way.

3. *Being able to "cut the cord"*—Some women have always dreamed of traveling the world; other women are miserable at the prospect of moving away from their parents. If you are of the latter, know that you can stay close to home if you develop a solid family strategy with your service member that plots out his career and identifies duty stations near home. Be aware, however, that circumstances may change and send your family off to Timbuktu—literally. If you simply cannot fathom the idea of being away from your hometown for two years, military life may not be for you.

4. *Asking for help when you need it*—Everyone needs help at some point in their lives. You are not alone. However, the worst thing you can do is refuse to get help while your crisis gets worse and worse. This is particularly true with regard to financial problems, depression, and domestic abuse. The military community is standing by with a cadre of financial counselors and free loans, psychiatrists and marital counselors, and the entire Family Advocacy Program to handle these issues, respectively. Similarly, there are approximately 700,000 active duty military wives—not to mention all the veteran wives—who know what you're going through and can lend a hand. Get help before your problem turns into a major crisis.

5. *Being your own woman*—Most marriages start out with the couple being exceptionally close. Yet with military life, deployment is a question of when—not whether—he will go. It takes a sense of independence and self-esteem to be able to handle life on your own again, and then reunite with your service member for an even more romantic and fulfilling marriage. The most experienced military wives I know actually look forward to deployment in some ways. They use the extra time and independence to take classes, spend

time with friends, and do fun things they otherwise wouldn't have time to do. Less successful military wives sit on the couch and mope. Which gal do you want to be?

6. *Never letting the system get the best of you*—Nothing is more irritating than women who play dumb and expect others to take care of things for them. Not only is this behavior obnoxious and self-demeaning, these women are also leaving their fate in the hands of people who really don't care. And then they wonder why their lives are so bad!

7. *Turning off CNN and listening to your command about information on your service member's safety*—Many newbie wives thrive on CNN because they think it will be the quickest way to get information about their deployed service member. They don't realize that the American news media is designed to sell one thing: drama. From this drama inevitably come speculation and rumors about what actually happened and how bad the situation really is. Don't fall into this trap! Turn off the television! It may be delayed, but your command admin or family support leader has more (and more detailed) information regarding your service member's exact status.

8. *Setting the standard of perfection*—Some women think they're cool by driving over the speed limit on base, dressing like prostitutes, and getting drunk at command functions. But this is not high school. You are socializing with your husband's bosses and colleagues, and you need to behave as such. You may be harming your service member's career prospects—and therefore your income potential!—by acting wildly. So grow up already!

I am convinced that all women of every personality type can succeed in military life. Sure, we all sometimes stray down the path of frustration and resentment. Who doesn't? Civilian life has its downsides, too. But in the end we can have the adventure of a lifetime. The question is: What kind of adventure will you have?

I look forward to hearing your cocktail party stories.

CHAPTER 14

Really Stupid Acronyms and Jargon

Okay, I admit that acronyms and jargon can be useful—and all wives and women in uniform must get to know them. But that doesn't mean the whole thing hasn't gotten out of control. Following are translations of the lingo that will serve you well.

AAFES—*Army and Air Force Exchange Service* (pronounced "a-fees"). Operates the Exchanges or department stores on Army and Air Force Bases. (See also "PX.")

ACS—*Army Community Services.* See "FSC."

AFB—*Air Force Base.* Example: "Lackland AFB in San Antonio, Texas."

AFRTS—*Armed Forces Radio and Television Services.* Military TV and radio.

AFSA—*Air Force Services Agency.* See "MWR."

AFTB—*Army Family Team Building.* An Army program to empower and encourage family members to be self-sufficient and mission-ready.

Allotment—An amount of money set aside from your monthly paycheck and paid directly to a specified individual. Many service members use an allotment to pay rent or creditors.

ANCOC—*Advanced Noncommissioned Officer Course.*

BAH—*Basic Allowance for Housing.* A key component of your pay that is supposed to cover the local cost of housing for either a single service member or a family.

BAS—*Basic Allowance for Subsistence.* The service member's food allowance.

Basic Pay—The main component of military pay. Based on pay grade.

BDU—*Battle Dress Uniform.* The Navy's term for a camouflage uniform. As if there isn't enough for a newbie to learn, the Navy refuses to call this uniform what it is. Many a newbie wife (and her husband) have been embarrassed at the uniform supply store over this term.

BHA—*Basic Housing Allowance.* See "BAH."

Billet—A Navy job or position handed down by the gods known as "detailers."

BNCOC—*Basic Noncommissioned Officer Course.*

BOQ/BEQ—*Bachelor Officer's Quarters/Bachelor Enlisted Quarters.* Where single officers, single enlisted, and geographical bachelors live. If space is available, where you and your husband may stay on vacations (other than the service lodges) on military sites, or where your husband stays while on a base deployment.

Branch Manager—The "Job Guy" in the Army who determines your soldier's next duty station.

BUPERS—The Navy's *Bureau of Personnel.*

BX—See "PX."

CDS—*Child Development Services.* Inexpensive day care on base.

CINC—Commander in Chief (pronounced "sink"), i.e., the President of the United States. The term used to refer to the highest-ranking commander in the theater of operation; for example, CINCPAC in the Pacific.

CinCHouse—*Commander in Chief of the House* (pronounced "sink house"). Jargon for the lady of the household and the ultimate authority to whom the service member reports. Sample use: "Soldier, I know you want to go on that spec ops mission to Outer Mongolia, but have you checked to see if that's okay with CinCHouse and the kids?"

CO—*Commanding Officer.* The head honcho of the unit.

COLA—*Cost of Living Adjustment.* An increase or decrease in pay, depending on how expensive or cheap it is to live in your area. COLA increases, for example, when you live overseas or in a city such as Washington, D.C. It bottoms out in places such as Jacksonville, North Carolina.

Commissary—The military-run grocery store on base. You can save up to 44 percent on groceries just by shopping there!

CONUS—*Continental United States.*

CPO—*Civilian Personnel Office.* The place to get a job with the government or on base.

DeCa—*Defense Commissary Agency.* See "Commissary."

DEERS—*Defense Enrollment Eligibility Reporting Service.* The personnel department of the military that determines which benefits you're entitled to.

Deploy—To go out on a mission for a lengthy period of time.

DEROS—*Date of Estimated Return from Overseas.* The big homecoming! When the service member is expected to return from an overseas assignment.

Detailer—The god (or demon) responsible for job and duty station assignments. Pay homage to this person, or be assigned to the hinterlands for a three-year tour.

DFAS—*Defense Finance and Accounting Service.* The bean counters of the Department of Defense and the folks responsible for paying you accurately.

DH—*Deployed or Darling Hubby.* Mostly an Internet thing.

DITY Move—*Do-It-Yourself move.* To relocate your household goods yourself, without the help of professional movers.

DLA—*Dislocation Allowance.* The pay you receive to cover the cost of relocation.

Duty Station—The location to which a service member is assigned to work. Also called "post," although "post" also can refer to the base itself. Confused yet?

ECHO—*Extended Care Health Option.* ECHO is a health insurance supplement to Tricare that covers additional costs associated with family members with special needs.

EFMP—*Exceptional Family Member Program.* EFMP status is given by a health care professional to a family member with special needs, and it gives that family member access to medical and other services.

ETS—*Expiration Term of Service.* The date the service member is scheduled to get out of the military unless he or she reenlists.

Exchange—See "PX."

FFSC—*Fleet & Family Support Center.* See "FSC."

FSC—*Family Support Center* or *Family Services Center.* The base office that helps military families with everything from relocation to financial counseling.

GS—*General Schedule.* Example: GS 9. Refers to the rank of a civilian government employee, with GS 1 being the lowest peon; you won't see anything much above GS 15.

High-3—One of two types of pension plans for military retirees. The other type is REDUX.

IA—*Individual Augmentation.* When a service member is pulled out of a command unexpectedly or given PCS orders to deploy to a duty station (usually in a combat zone) where he will "augment" a new unit. This has become similar to a one-year unaccompanied tour, but nearly always in a combat zone.

ITT—*Information, Tickets, & Tours.* A great place to get cheap tickets for rock concerts, movies, and even Disneyland!

Key Volunteer—A family support group leader (usually a wife) for a unit in the Marine Corps.

LES—*Leave and Earnings Statement.* Your monthly pay stub, which also happens to tell you how much vacation (leave) time the service member has.

L.I.N.K.S.—*Lifestyle Insights Networking Knowledge and Skills.* This is the Marine Corps version of AFTB, where they teach the basics of getting around the green side, how to read an LES, where things are on your base, how to survive life as a military (Marine) spouse, and more.

MCB—*Marine Corps Base.* Example: "MCB Camp Pendleton."

MCCS—*Marine Corps Community Services.* See "FSC" and "MWR."

MCX—See "PX."

MRE—*Meals Ready to Eat.* The crappy freeze-dried meal that your husband will talk about when he gets back from hardship deployment. Best seasoned by Taco Bell hot sauce packets sent in care packages.

MTF—*Military Treatment Facility.* A military hospital or health care clinic.

MWR—*Morale, Welfare, and Recreation.* This office is like that of the Cruise Director on the *Love Boat*: always full of ideas on fun things to do.

NB—*Naval Base.* Example: "NB San Diego."

NCO—*Noncommissioned Officer.* Enlisted senior management.

NCOIC—*Noncommissioned Officer in Charge.*

O Club—*The Officers' Club.* Official restaurant and bar of the officers. The enlisted have their own club, although many bases are integrating both clubs into one. Officers and enlisted are not allowed to be overly social with one another because of the need to maintain professional boundaries. So they let it all hang out when they're among their own ranks.

OCONUS—*Outside the Continental United States.* Overseas; or Hawaii or Puerto Rico.

OCS—*Officer Candidate School.* Where newly recruited officer candidates in the Army, Navy, USMC, Air Force, and Coast Guard must spend approximately 13 weeks without their families to learn the ways of the military and to qualify as a commissioned officer. They will come back spouting acronyms and probably make up a few of their own.

OIC—*Officer in Charge.* The guy to call when you can't find your husband in an emergency.

OIS—*Officer Indoctrination School.* The diet version of OCS.

Ombudsman—A family support group leader (usually a wife) for a command in the Navy.

OOC—*Out of Commission.* I.e., "broken." Don't ask why they can't just say "broken."

Orders—A written instruction (piece of paper) from the military for a service member to leave his command and to go to a new job. Your orders indicate the dates when the service member will separate from his old command and when he is due at his new command, as well as information on the relocation process.

OTC—*Officer Training Course.* Same as Officer Candidate School but for the Air Force.

Pay Grade—The category that determines your service member's level of Basic Pay. Pay grade is tied to rank. Thus, an Air Force Airman and a Navy Seaman Apprentice both have a pay grade of E-2. An Army Major and a Navy Lieutenant Commander both have a pay grade of O-4.

PCM—*Primary Care Manager.* Your main doctor chosen or assigned by Tricare.

PCS—*Permanent Change of Station.* The term is actually used as the verb "to relocate." Example: "My family is PCSing to Japan. It's a really big move for us!"

Per Diem—The pay a service member receives each day to cover the cost of travel while on temporary duty.

PLDC—*Primary Leadership Developmental Course.* For enlisted personnel.

POA—*Power of Attorney.* A legal document that allows you to conduct business on behalf of your service member in his absence. Don't let him leave home without giving you one!

POTUS—*President of the United States.* This term is reserved for a president you really hate, and it was often used for President Clinton, who was generally disliked by the military community. Most presidents are referred to as "Commander in Chief."

POV—*Personally Owned Vehicle.* Your car or truck.

PSD—*Personnel Support Detachment.* Consider it the company personnel department.

PT—*Physical Training.* Usually the morning exercises required by each command.

PX—*Post Exchange* (in Army terms). The department store on base. The Marines call it "MCX," the Air Force calls it "BX," and the Navy calls it "Exchange." If you're not confused already, it is also referred to as "AAFES" (pronounced "a-fees") because it is operated by the Army and Air Forces Exchange System.

QTRS—*Quarters.* Your living area, a.k.a. house or apartment.

Rank—The title and level at which your service member has been promoted in the military hierarchy. For example, a Marine who passed boot camp has earned the title of Private and later can be promoted to Private First Class, then Lance Corporal, and so on. Rank is tied to pay grade, which determines your service member's level of Basic Pay.

REDUX—One of two types of pension plans for military retirees. The other type is High-3.

Relocation—The move of your household to a new place.

RIF—*Reduction in Force.* Layoffs with honorable discharge. Not necessarily a bad thing if you get a good separation bonus.

SBP—*Survivor Benefit Plan.* The pittance you get as a widow if he dies.

SCOR—*Specialized Care Organizational Record.* The consolidated records you should keep for an EFMP family member with special needs.

SGLI—*Service Members' Group Life Insurance.* The inexpensive term life insurance plan provided by the Department of Defense.

Space A—*Space Available.* Refers to remaining seats on military transport planes that are available for service members and families to travel for leisure or relocation.

TDY or **TAD**—*Temporary Duty/Temporary Assigned Duty.* Temporary assignment to a station or post, usually a training program. Spouse and family are typically not allowed to accompany a service member unless they pay for it out of their own pocket.

Threatcon—*Threat Condition.* The level of security on base that determines how much the gate guards will harass you. Threatcon Alpha means we are at war and you are not allowed on base unless you live there.

Tricare—The military's very own HMO.

TSP—*Thrift Savings Plan.* A retirement savings plan every service member should participate in.

Unaccompanied Tour—A permanent duty station in which the service member's family is not allowed to relocate or live with the service member. These tours are usually in remote, difficult locations, such as South Korea or islands in the Indian Ocean, and last for one year.

USA—*United States Army.* Gotcha! You'd think they'd find a different acronym.

XO—*Executive Officer.* Second in command to the Commanding Officer (CO) and usually the "bad" guy (disciplinarian) of the unit.

ACKNOWLEDGMENTS

Here's a shout-out to my husband, Fernando, for his endless support of my career, attentive sharing in my hopes and fears, and non-stop strategizing. I completed the original edition of this book just before giving birth to our son, Alex. Two weeks and three sets of grandparents later, Fernando watched Alex nearly full-time while I banged out edits for an early pub date. I can't thank him enough for being my partner in life.

I want to thank my parents who, bizarrely enough, continue to wonder who taught me that I can do anything I put my mind to. I learned from the best!

Special thanks go to my agent Kristen Auclair and editor Shawna Lietzke. You took a chance on us li'l ole military wives, and we all won—especially the newbie wives who need it the most. Thank you also for the endless plotting and scheming about how we can conquer the world together. The office-chair jig has become my favorite new dance.

Most important, thank you to the military wives and women in uniform on CinCHouse and around the world for your endless support, ideas, questions, and inspiration. *Married to the Military* is truly the amalgamation of your advice and experience. Congratulations on a job well done!

INDEX